Springer Series in Design and Innovation

Volume 15

Editor-in-Chief

Francesca Tosi, University of Florence, Florence, Italy

Series Editors

Claudio Germak, Politecnico di Torino, Turin, Italy

Francesco Zurlo, Politecnico di Milano, Milan, Italy

Zhi Jinyi, Southwest Jiaotong University, Chengdu, China

Marilaine Pozzatti Amadori, Universidade Federal de Santa Maria, Santa Maria, Rio Grande do Sul, Brazil

Maurizio Caon, University of Applied Sciences and Arts, Fribourg, Switzerland

Alessandro Deserti · Marion Real ·
Felicitas Schmittinger
Editors

Co-creation for Responsible Research and Innovation

Experimenting with Design Methods and Tools

Editors
Alessandro Deserti 
Department of Design
Politecnico di Milano
Milan, Italy

Marion Real
Fab Lab Barcelona
Barcelona, Spain

Felicitas Schmittinger
Department of Design
Politecnico di Milano
Milan, Italy

ISSN 2661-8184   ISSN 2661-8192 (electronic)
Springer Series in Design and Innovation
ISBN 978-3-030-78735-6   ISBN 978-3-030-78733-2 (eBook)
https://doi.org/10.1007/978-3-030-78733-2

This Springer imprint is published by the registered company Springer Nature Switzerland AG
The registered company address is: Gewerbestrasse 11, 6330 Cham, Switzerland

Preface

The relationship between science, technology and society is being rethought towards logics of permeability and dialogue, rendering the needs, desires and expectations of the latter as important drivers for innovation. A paradigmatic shift concerning the role of citizens in science, research and innovation is witnessed, as well as in Science, Technology and Innovation (STI) policymaking. In particular, the discourse on public engagement and Responsible Research and Innovation (RRI) powerfully became a matter of spread interest, showing the need of models that lead to an effective integration of co-design and bottom-up co-creation initiatives for encouraging/stimulating scientific and technological advancement as the result of a synergic, inclusive cooperation among actors that usually work autonomously. To address the topic, 17 cross-sector partners from all over Europe started the three-year EU-funded project SISCODE (Society in Innovation and Science through CO-DEsign). Interconnecting an analysis of the theoretical background and existing cases with real-life experimentations (RLEs), the investigation sets up a reflective and learning framework to explore the transformations in initiatives and policies emerging from the interaction between citizens and stakeholders.

The book presents a critical analysis of the co-design processes activated in 10 co-creation laboratories addressing societal challenges across Europe. Each laboratory as a case study of a RLE is described through its journey, starting from the purpose on the ground of the experimentation and the challenge addressed. Specific attention is then drawn on the role of policies and policymaker engagement. Finally, the experimentation is enquired in terms of its output, transformations triggered within the organisation and the overall ecosystem, and its outcomes, opening the reasoning towards the lessons learnt and reflections that the entire co-creation journey brought.

Milan, Italy   Alessandro Deserti
Barcelona, Spain   Marion Real
Milan, Italy   Felicitas Schmittinger

Contents

Between Science, Technology and Society

Alessandro Deserti and Francesca Rizzo

The intersection and permeability of science, innovation and society result in a series of benefits and challenges, underlying the important role the latter can and should play. The following paragraphs present the theoretical background and the objectives of the SISCODE (**S**ociety in **I**nnovation and **S**cience through **CO-DE**sign) project investigating this interconnection, the issues that emerged through its journey and the results gained. Therefore, it frames the knowledge obtained throughout the three-year duration of the project, situating the notion of Responsible Research and Innovation (RRI) in the co-creation domain, and introducing the issues that emerge when moving from the theoretical concept to practice [1, 2]. It inspects how co-creation and design knowledge and tools can be applied to engage citizens in shaping solutions that are meant to be more inclusive, responsible and sustainable, and how these approaches and methodologies could be applied to operationalize RRI. Particular attention is drawn to how small-scale experimentations can lead to significant scale-in, scale-up and scale-out processes. The book will show how these processes can lead to organizational learning and transformation, but also how they can provide evidence-based knowledge which nurtures policy making processes with the potential of achieving broader societal impacts in Science, Technology and Innovation (STI) policy making [3]. Investigating the benefits and implications of applying participatory research and innovation approaches in society, this chapter embraces a context-sensitive perspective [4] and explores the crossroads of diverse forms of innovation: not only research-driven but also practice-based, and not only technological but also social. This reasoning provided the theoretical background which led to the construction of a learning framework, adopted as a guide for the 10 co-creation labs in which the real-life experimentations described in this volume were conducted.

A. Deserti (✉) · F. Rizzo
Department of Design, Politecnico di Milano, 20158 Milan, Italy
e-mail: alessandro.deserti@polimi.it

© The Author(s) 2022
A. Deserti et al. (eds.), *Co-creation for Responsible Research and Innovation*,
Springer Series in Design and Innovation 15,
https://doi.org/10.1007/978-3-030-78733-2_1

1   Areas of Interest of the SISCODE Project

SISCODE combined diverse fields of study and areas of work. In particular, the research and innovation project investigated the relationship between RRI and co-creation, with a specific focus on STI policy making. These distinct matters have been reconnected in theory and practice, identifying a potentiality of achieving positive results and impacts when applying co-creation approaches, methodologies and tools to operationalize RRI [5].

Responsible Research and Innovation

Innovation and science are powerful drivers when it comes to the development of all factors that influence modern society and therefore the direction of transformation of societies and all the single individuals that are a part of it [6]. The recognition of this influence has led to the emergence of a new approach in the fields of science, research and innovation, to make them more responsible impacting STI policy making. The emergence of the approach within the framework and context of European policy making dates back to 2011 having been introduced as a top-down approach for research policy which contrasts with the concept itself promoting bottom-up initiatives and pathways to innovation [7].

RRI entails the transition from solutions developed internally within the research community and only tolerated passively by society towards ones that are taking citizens and other actors actively into consideration as part of the development of solutions that are more apt to achieve desirable results with a high impact [6].

This reflection on the societal impact of innovation calls for a change in innovation processes and a shift of roles of its actors, including all players into the innovation process, which should lead to sharing and redefining power, privileges and responsibilities [2]. Apart from the aspect of inclusion, RRI aims to anticipate impacts by analyzing the contexts of implementation and taking into account all the actors and factors that influence the implementation of a solution. Furthermore, findings throughout the development are planned to impact on the process itself, making it more reflective, flexible and responsive to new insights and perspectives [8].

Witnessing this shift towards the involvement of citizens and other actors in the innovation process, it is necessary to understand its potentialities as well as its implications: this calls for new approaches, techniques, processes and mindsets for the effective integration and involvement of society in innovation.

Despite having been widely discussed in theory as a relevant opportunity to move towards more sustainable futures [9], there's still a lack of evidence of impacts of RRI in empirical settings, which leaves open issues especially in terms of context-sensitivity and translation from theory into practice for real and measurable impact [10].

It has been recognized that the full adoption of RRI requires an in-depth transformation in organizations and ecosystems or institutional settings, to be embedded as a general approach towards innovation that requires the reflection not only on the outcomes of innovation itself but also the purpose and process of innovating leading to a shift in the overall mindset and way of working.

The scientific and technological advancement and the responsibility related to it discussed in RRI directly refers to the substantial societal challenges that are being tackled with innovation [2].

Co-creation

Co-creation has received significant attention in the context of innovation in recent years, in particular as a part of the field of participatory design. It has been identified as a potential booster for the implementation of new and experimental solutions due to both its practicality and its versatility in adapting to diverse and changing environments and contexts [11].

One of the central points of co-creation is the transformation of passive actors like end-users into operating ones, involving them actively in the development processes of products, services and systems [12] to define and create value commonly and taking all actors and their needs into account [13].

Co-creation considers users and actors not only during research phases, but aims to actively involve them across the phases of ideation in co-design processes until the prototyping and implementation of a solution, thus including co-production [14].

From a business point of view, this active involvement in participatory processes usually aims at the co-creation of value, shifting the focus from a business-centric one towards personalised and satisfying customer experiences [15].

These characteristics led to expanding the fields of application as well as the notion of co-creation. In particular, it has been experimented as a promising means to engage neglected actors and stakeholders in other fields of innovation (e.g. in public sector innovation) and as a way to set up collaborative processes like those that are needed to better include society in innovation [5].

The SISCODE project explored this pathway of operationalizing RRI through co-creation to investigate the potentialities, opportunities and barriers of co-creation in the RRI context. In particular, the project analysed the favorable conditions for co-creation, the dynamics activated during the process of adoption of co-creation, and how capacities for co-creation in organisations are built.

2 The SISCODE Project and Its Objectives

SISCODE (Society in Innovation and Science through CO-DEsign) is a three-year EU-funded project within the Horizon 2020 programme with 17 cross-sector partners, completed in April 2021.

It aimed to explore the application of co-creation, and co-design specifically, for the operationalization of RRI in different contexts.

Its investigation is based on the triangulation of the results of different but inter-connected research streams: the theoretical framing of the single areas of work (primarily RRI, co-creation and policy making) and their interconnection; the anal-ysis of existing cases where co-creation has been applied in the context of RRI in Europe and beyond; and finally, the conduction of ten real-life experimentations. For the conduction of the experimentation, an analytical, reflective learning framework was developed to explore the provoked shifts and transformations in projects and organizations, as well as in policies and policy making processes triggered by the interaction between citizens, stakeholders and policy makers. Therefore, the project frames the knowledge obtained throughout the three years of the project, situating the notion of RRI in the co-creation domain, and introducing issues that emerge when moving from the theoretical concept to practice [1, 2].

Objectives

To grasp and further explore the circulation and establishing of the phenomenon of co-creation as an approach for bottom-up and design-driven development as well as its potential for replication and scaling when applied in the context of RRI, the SISCODE project was carried out according to three main objectives:

1. The production of a study extended across Europe to investigate existing co-creation ecosystems at different scales ranging from local and regional to national levels and identify and extract patterns of dynamics, drivers and barriers encountered when integrating society in science and innovation. It specifically addressed the cultural, organisational, institutional and regulatory conditions that may favour or hinder co-creation. Furthermore, particular attention was posed to the engagement of stakeholders, the techniques and dynamics of their involvement and how their diversity influenced and affected the process and the final solution.
2. The experimentation of (co-)design not only as an approach, but also as a set of skills and competences, to see how the building of these capacities can be favoured and supported to enable the application co-creation in RRI and STI policy making.
3. The understanding of the transformation needed beyond the development of capacities in terms of organisational, procedural and cultural shifts for the permanent and stable embedding of co-creation in organisational processes and culture and how eventual barriers identified can be overcome.

In essence, SISCODE aimed to explore the operationalization of RRI by investigating the application of co-creation to reach this goal, starting from the theoretical background and existing cases to then conduct its own transnational experimentation across Europe.

This book describes this system of co-creation labs and provides insights drawn from their experimentation of applying co-creation in their single contexts while being in constant exchange with each other, with the networks that they created to conduct the experimentation and with the other partners in the research consortium, to foster peer-to-peer learning and cross-fertilisation.

3 RRI in SISCODE—From Theory to Practice through Co-creation

SISCODE investigated how knowledge, methodologies and tools from the field of design can be applied to shape concrete solutions to relevant societal challenges towards Responsible Innovation taking the inclusivity, responsibility and sustainability of these solutions into account.

The activities conducted are aimed to function as a bridge for the identified gap between theory and practice in RRI through the collaborative development of specific solutions.

In these processes, citizens and other stakeholders are engaged to collaboratively develop solutions for specific local and global problems. The research project investigated and reflected upon the broader transformations triggered by the experimentations and the exchange within the project, both at an organisational level of the single labs as well as within their surrounding ecosystem.

Co-creation has been applied as a means to deal with and overcome the barriers identified in the operationalization of RRI and to trigger the shift within organisations needed to fully embed the new approach to then influence the entire ecosystem.

A series of activities were planned and conducted to support these processes in the frame of the project and provide concrete support to the pilots:

- **Training**
  Knowledge on co-creation was transmitted in specific training sessions, providing background knowledge, tools for the conduction of co-creation activities, like canvases, cards and instruction, and building capacities for the planning, conduction and facilitation of workshops and other co-creation activities.
- **Opportunities for peer-to-peer learning**
  Acknowledging the diversity of the pilots and the influence of these differences and the entirely distinct contexts, confrontation has been identified as an opportunity to exchange best practices, ideas and collaboratively find solutions to specific problems. For this reason, regular meetings and calls have been organised as a space for interrelation, conversation and peer-to-peer learning.
- **Dialogue between researchers and practitioners**
  Recognizing the gap between theory and practice not only identified in literature but in the project itself among academic partners and practitioners, a series of meetings have been organised to discuss specific research topics from the various points of view, aiming to bridge this gap within the project and identifying points of connection and dialogue between researchers and practitioners.
- **Reporting as an instrument for self-reflection**
  Material to be produced for reporting and assessing the experimentation has been mainly collected following templates composed by a series of reflective questions to trigger reflections on the conducted activities and ongoing transformations while reporting them.

A learning framework, described in detail in Chap. 2, was set up to support and guide this process of moving from theory to practice having all pilots following the same general framework adapting its elements to the specific context and conditions. This is relevant in terms of reacting to the previously identified importance of the context while preserving the possibility to still assess and compare the single experimentations notwithstanding their diversity.

The overall project adopted an approach to place these small-scale experiments within larger ecosystems of co-creation exploring opportunities for scaling and reconnect the findings to the general issues identified during the initial desk research.

4 The Importance of Small-Scale Experiments

The necessity of impacting ecosystems on a broader scale to influence policies requires impact at not only local, but regional, national and international levels [16]. Small-scale pilots have been identified as a potential to experiment new approaches and concepts to then 'scale, what works' [17].

The advantage of pilots conducted on a smaller scale is not only related to their feasibility but also to their focus on a limited and very specific environment adopting a sensitive perspective in relation to the surrounding context [4]. This context-sensitivity becomes particularly relevant when investigating RRI initiatives where significant levels of context-dependence have been found as one of the barriers for implementation [13, 18–20].

This aspect underlines both the importance of small-scale experiments conducted in very specific contexts to then make considerations on their scaling as well as the necessity to consider these scaling processes and integrate them into pilots like the ones conducted in SISCODE from the very beginning.

Moore et al. have divided the scaling process into three different elements, scaling up, scaling out and scaling deep, and all three of them combined are necessary to impact larger systems [16].

- **Scaling out** refers to the wider dissemination and replication of the solution to impact a larger number of addressants in this way [16]. In SISCODE, this dimension has been addressed with a variety of dissemination activities in each lab together with business model workshops and considerations on replication to reflect and collect feedback on opportunities of scaling the single solutions out beyond the project context.
- **Scaling up** relates directly to the influence on laws and policies transforming existing institutions [16]. The pilots have addressed this dimension seeking direct contact, exchange and confrontation specifically with policy makers and decision makers in their respective field of work to collaboratively understand barriers and opportunities within the current policy framework together with potentialities to influence and transform this framework participating and contributing in the shaping of new policies.

Here it is worth to be mentioned, that especially the value of evidence-based knowledge has been explored to reach out to decision makers to achieve broader impacts on society.

- **Scaling deep** introduces culture and mindset as an additional dimension to be influenced to achieve impact at a greater scale. The cultural and visionary shift that is required to deeply embed a new solution, its mindset and approach to ensure not only its integration in a context but also create a fertile ground for replication and scaling with the involved actors eventually becoming advocates to further distribute innovation.

Particular attention has been posed at this dimension in SISCODE investigating the changes in mindset and way of working, that the pilot has triggered both in the organisation and the surrounding ecosystem together with the dynamics of these transformations.

5 Levels and Dimensions of Investigation

The specific levels investigated in SISCODE range from the micro and meso up to the macro level. While the micro level refers to the internal activities and dynamics as well as the immediate surroundings of an organisation, the meso level zooms out to networks of stakeholders and bigger groups often still limited to a regional level, while the macro level takes a focus on national and institutional governance processes up to transnational dynamics and systems [21].

While the experimentations did mainly take place and directly impacted on a micro-level, the project explored and reflected on how each of the experimental solutions could be scaled or replicated to influence systems on meso- and even macro levels.

These levels of analysis are taken up in the final chapter, the comparative analysis, where the ten experimentations conducted are compared identifying essential differences and common aspects with a specific focus on policies and policy making when applying co-creation in RRI contexts, reconnecting them to the theoretical background of the project by drawing initial conclusions on barriers and opportunities considering a wider scale from a future perspective.

The following chapter presents the empirical reasoning at the ground of the experimentation and its methodology with the learning framework set up to plan, conduct and monitor the pilots. In particular, it shows how the process has been established to support the tackling of challenges for the single organisations in terms of stakeholder engagement, dealing with communities and society and managing transformations.

References

1. Von Schomberg L, Blok V (2018) The turbulent age of innovation. Synthese, pp 1–17

2. Von Schomberg R (2013) A vision of responsible research and innovation. In: Owen R, Bessant J, Heintz M (eds) Responsible innovation. Wiley, Chichester, pp 51–74
3. Deserti A, Rizzo F, Smallman M (2020) Experimenting with co-design in STI policy making. Policy Des Pract 3(2):135–149
4. Bekkers V, Tummers LG, Stuijfzand BG, Voorberg W (2013) Social innovation in the public sector: an integrative framework. LIPSE Working articles, 1
5. Bajmócy Z, Pataki G (2019) Responsible research and innovation and the challenge of co-creation. In: Responsible research and innovation and the challenge of co-creation (in press)
6. Owen R, Bessant J, Heintz M (eds) (2013) Responsible innovation: managing the responsible emergence of science and innovation in society. Wiley, Chichester
7. Zwart H, Landeweerd L, van Rooij A (2014) Adapt or perish? Assessing the recent shift in the European research funding arena from 'ELSA' to 'RRI.' Life Sci, Soc Policy 10(1):1–19
8. Stilgoe J, Owen R, Macnaghten P (2013) Developing a framework for responsible innovation. Res Policy 42:1568–1580
9. European Commission: Responsible research and innovation. https://ec.europa.eu/programmes/horizon2020/en/h2020-section/responsible-research-innovation. Last accessed 2021/03/28
10. European Commission (2015) Directorate-general for research and innovation: indicators for promoting and monitoring responsible research and innovation: report from the expert group on policy indicators for responsible research and innovation. Publications Office, Luxembourg
11. Payne AF, Storbacka K, Frow P (2008) Managing the co-creation of value. J Acad Mark Sci 36(1):83–96
12. Saarijärvi H (2012) The mechanisms of value co-creation. J Strateg Mark 20:381–391
13. Rizzo F, Deserti A, Komatsu TT (2020) Implementing social innovation in real contexts. Int J Knowl Based Dev 11(1):45–67
14. Frow P, Nenonen S, Payne A, Storbacka K (2015) Managing co-creation design: a strategic approach to innovation: managing co-creation design. Br J Manag 26(3):463–483
15. Prahalad CK, Ramaswamy V (2004) Co-creation experiences: the next practice in value creation. J Interact Mark 18:5–14
16. Moore M-L, Riddell D, Vocisano D (2015) Scaling out, scaling up, scaling deep: strategies of non-profits in advancing systemic social innovation. The J Corp Citizensh 58:67–84
17. Bradach J, Grindle A (2014) Emerging pathways to transformative scale. In: Smarter philanthropy for greater impact: rethinking how grantmakers support scale. Supplement to 'Stanford Social Innovation Review.'
18. Deserti A, Rizzo F (2019) Embedding design in the organizational culture: challenges and perspectives. In: Design culture: objects and approaches, pp 39–51
19. Deserti A, Rizzo F (2019) Context dependency of social innovation: in search of new sustainability models. Eur Plan Stud 28(5):864–880
20. Howlett M (2014) From the 'old' to the 'new' policy design: design thinking beyond markets and collaborative governance. Policy Sci 47(3):187–207
21. Rizzo F, Deserti A, Crabu S, Smallman M, Hjort J, Hansen SJ, Menichinelli M (2018) Co-creation in RRI practices and STI policies. SISCODE deliverable D1.2. https://ec.europa.eu/research/participants/documents/downloadPublic?documentIds=080166e5bedc3a0d&appId=PPGMS. Last accessed 2021/03/21.

A Framework for Experimenting Co-creation in Real-Life Contexts

Marion Real and Felicitas Schmittinger

The chapter describes the methodology applied throughout the experimentation, the application of co-design, the tools used and their role briefly illustrating the single cases. The underlying assumption is that design methodologies and tools are more suitable to support co-creation for the inclusion of society in science and innovation since their aim is to implement co-creation processes from the ideation of new products, services and processes to their real implementation. What differentiates design from other co-creation methodologies is the role of prototypes and their experimentation in real contexts.

1 Introduction

In the following the results of a practice-based approach are presented that aims to tackle the challenges of active actor engagement, the effective integration of co-creation in STI policymaking, and the operationalisation of RRI practices. In this context, exploring those practices in real-life opens up the possibilities to cope with constraints, identify new opportunities and explore ways to effectively embed co-creation.

The reasoning is situated in a context where many barriers are still in place, hindering the development of ecosystems of co-creation aimed at better inclusion of society in science and innovation. Still, the situation is evolving, pushed by a

M. Real (✉)
IAAC, Fab Lab Barcelona, Barcelona, Spain
e-mail: marion@fablabbcn.org

F. Schmittinger
Department of Design, Politecnico di Milano, 20158 Milan, Italy
e-mail: felicitas.schmittinger@polimi.it

© The Author(s) 2022

A. Deserti et al. (eds.), *Co-creation for Responsible Research and Innovation*,
Springer Series in Design and Innovation 15,
https://doi.org/10.1007/978-3-030-78733-2_2

growing interest towards co-creation that led to its integration in European research and innovation policies. Looking at the bigger picture, however, some of the main obstacles need to be outlined that researchers and practitioners are encountering when addressing RRI in practice. First of all, there is a general lack of awareness and understanding of the potentialities of co-creation among researchers, innovators, intermediaries and policymakers. The STI approach to policymaking, to which RRI is bounded, is known for being "sectorialised". This hampers collaboration among sectors and organisations. However, one of the main hindrances is the shortage of competences and methodologies to rely on for filling the gap between constructing solutions and policies and their real implementation. Eventually, there is a scarcity of learning frameworks to sustain and encourage the replication of co-creation mechanisms. In consequence, the main need of a framework able to include and leverage practical knowledge on how to cope with those constraints and barriers that come along during co-creation processes and their implementation has been identified.

In many fields, Design has been already recognised as a key actor in operationalising co-creation. Especially, co-design and its iterative cycles of understanding, ideating, prototyping, and verifying, resulted in successfully supporting co-creation along the process, that is to say from the ideation of new solutions and policies to their real implementation. In doing so, especially prototypes stood for contributing in bridging the gap between co-production and its outcomes. This is made possible by prototypes' ability to trigger and feed processes of real implementation where to experience all the aspects that come along when designing solutions. On a smaller, but real scale, everything is experiences: from coping with resources available, need and interests, conflicts with opportunities and barriers, organisational cultures and values, and larger cultural, institutional and regulatory frameworks. Such an inherent feature constitutes a strong rationale for understanding the potentialities as well as the implications of co-creation as a design-driven approach for better including society in science and innovation. Moreover, in the light of the main obstacles depicted above, especially building an evidence-based learning framework becomes paramount, allowing for the integration of co-creation with larger STI governance systems.

In this volume, other than exploring the theoretical background of co-design in RRI and analysing existing cases of the application of co-design in a European context and beyond, conducting RLEs is a way for grasping concrete and situated knowledge about a complex interaction where several actors participate throughout the entire process. These actors can be either members of the organisation conducting the experimentation or external to this organisation, but are relevant actors in the context of the activity. These actors can be users of a product or service or stakeholders of its delivery. Potential stakeholders can be public institutions, enterprises or policymakers.

To advance knowledge on the topic, a set of field experimentations were conducted and monitored purposely identified as cross-disciplinary and varied in their nature. The results and outcomes obtained from such high-impact experiments in real-life contexts allowed to gather concrete knowledge on the operationalisation of RRI and the integration of co-creation in STI policymaking. By engaging citizens, local actors, stakeholders such as policymakers and the wider scientific community, the experimentation has the objective to increase knowledge on co-creation through action research [1]. At the same time, the effectiveness of design methodologies is tested to better combine co-construction or ideation with the co-production or actual implementation of the ideated solutions and policies for the integration of society in science and innovation.

Those experiments took place in 10 co-creation labs across Europe, each of them is a member of one of three following networks that will be described in detail later on:

- The Fab City Foundation managed in part by Fab Lab Barcelona,
- The European Network of Living Labs (ENoLL), and
- The European network of Science Centres and Museums (ECSITE).

The three networks as a system of trans-national collectors and areas of encounter and exchange for their member labs provided first insights on co-creative environments within their networks. They contributed already in the initial phase of the project with drivers and barriers previously identified by their members regarding the effectiveness of the above-mentioned co-creation approaches, processes and tools; during the ongoing experimentation they actively supported their respective members in their journeys.

Although the experimentation was initially supposed to last around 18 months, the period has been extended to 21 due to the manifold restriction caused by the Covid pandemic. In these experiments, each lab tackled a specific societal challenge and engaged a set of stakeholders in a co-creation process. from the stage of co-design where stakeholders will analyse the context, reframe the problem and envision alternatives, to that of co-production of prototypes within an iterative process.

The following sections detail the approach to co-creation on the base of the experimentation consisting in a learning framework and process guideline and an accompanying, modular toolbox. Furthermore, the objectives of this approach are illustrated in detail together with the single labs and networks and how their experimentations have been both supported and assessed throughout the process.

2 SISCODE Approach to Co-creation

Co-creation is approached in this volume as a design-driven and currently flourishing phenomenon across Europe occurring in bottom-up initiatives like innovation labs, social innovation initiatives, communities, and regions.

The experimentation aims to analyse significant conditions for the successful introduction, scaling and replication of co-creation practices while cross-pollinating RRI initiatives and the field of policymaking [2]. To achieve this, the approach applied throughout the experimentation is using design practices and processes as a base for the development of a process and attributive tools to build capacities and competences for the implementation of RRI and STI policymaking [3]. This approach consists in a learning framework and a toolbox specifically developed for the RLE conducted aiming to overcome barriers and resistances to change. Both the organisation at the core of the initiative as well as all the external actors and stakeholders involved in the development are considered and targeted by this approach.

Experience-based learning framework
The way SISCODE looks at co-creation is seeing it as "a non-linear process that involves multiple actors and stakeholders in the ideation, implementation and assessment of products, services, policies and systems with the aim of improving their efficiency and effectiveness, and the satisfaction of those who take part in the process" [1, 3, 4]. The integrated core structure of the design processes can be complemented with appropriate tools associated to one or more phases to support the co-creation of new solutions while the (organisational) learning process can be complemented with appropriate structures and actions, and applied to the introduction and integration of new knowledge.

By interpreting an organisation not only as a structure closed in itself but as an actor in a greater network where other actors like municipalities, public services or enterprises play their function and relate, the learning process can be extended to all those actors being actively involved in the learning process through the application of the principles of co-design [5].

In the light of this reasoning, to develop the theoretical framework at the ground of the experimentation Kolb's cycle of experiential learning [6] has been combined with the iterative process of co-design. The scheme below represents the framework integrating experimentation and learning. This framework will be used to connect the activities conducted in the 10 co-creation labs with policymakers at local, regional, national, and EU levels (Fig. 1).

The developed learning cycle basically foresees four stages within an iterative process:

- Concrete Experience: the learner encounters a new experience or situation, or reinterprets an existing experience.
- Reflective Observation: the learner reflects on the experience on a personal basis, trying to map the gap between experience and understanding.
- Abstract Conceptualisation: the learner elaborates new ideas based on the previous reflection or on modifications of the existing abstract ideas. This phase focuses on envisioning alternatives.
- Active Experimentation: the learner applies the new ideas to his/her surroundings to see if there are any modifications in the next appearance of the experience.

Beginning from the analysis of the context to then move from the reframing of the initially defined problem and the envisioning of alternatives into an iterative cycle itself of developing and prototyping. In the following each phase is detailed, pointing out their main features and output.

Analysis of the context
The phase of context analysis has the scope of providing the space and instruments needed to clearly define the context in which the chosen challenge is addressed with a

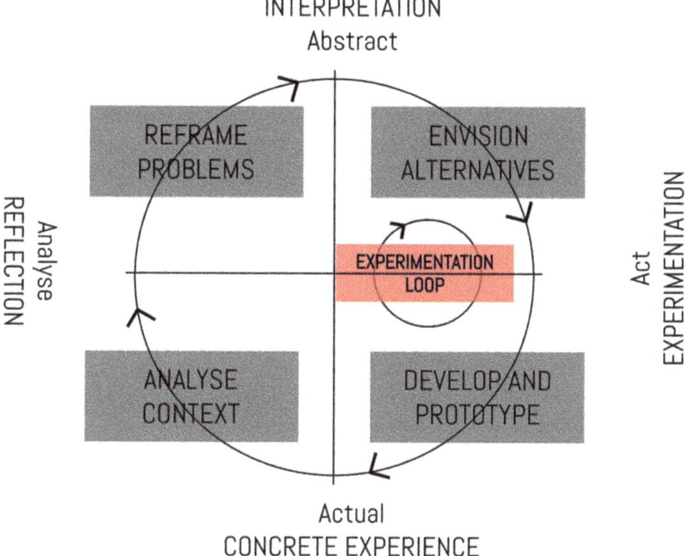

Fig. 1 The design-based learning framework

focus on specific local particularities, stakeholders, and current policies. Defining the context through research is meant to form the base to explore the relation between the context and the challenge itself, as well as to clarify the competences that the lab needs to be able to frame and define the problem. Since this first phase, the involvement of a variety of stakeholders and users is already required with them being part of the ecosystem in which the lab operates. The aim is to obtain a complete picture of the context and needs of the various actors: such knowledge is in fact key to precisely frame the problem.

Problem framing

The precise definition of the root of the problem is essential for the ideation of an efficient and effective solution. Moreover it is necessary to consider that the initial challenge might be linked to other, greater problems underneath, which have to be acknowledged and tackled all together in order to provoke real change.

This phase is entirely dedicated to the understanding of the problem, its roots and the influencing factors. As in the first phase of context analysis, the active participation of stakeholders is fundamental to explore not only influencing factors, but also different perspectives from which the problem could be seen. This is crucial to gain a multi-perspective view and a complete understanding of the problem itself.

Envisioning solutions

Moving from problems to opportunities and solutions during the third phase, the detailed challenge and needs defined previously are addressed to improve the current situation. This phase is dedicated to ideating potential solutions imagining an ideal scenario in which the problem is solved.

Building the ideal scenario itself and reasoning on its elements can already be a starting point for the gathering of new ideas. To keep the variety of points of view and needs to be satisfied the involvement of stakeholders needs to be kept consistent also throughout this step. The presence of multiple perspectives leads to shaping a value proposition from the different ideas generated.

Developing and prototyping

The last phase of the journey is dedicated to the application of the newly developed concepts to turn them into implementable prototypes. The prototypes designed are then tested and assessed through an iterative process aimed at identifying the best possible solution step by step together with users and concerned actors.

As illustrated in Fig. 2, the framework is presented as cyclical, emphasising the importance of iteration when designing and experimenting in real-life.

In addition to this learning model, a toolbox has been developed to operationalise and support the learning effect and favor capacity building in a variety of contexts.

The toolbox

The toolbox has been created as an open set of tools to operationalise the single phases of the learning framework to facilitate both the design and the implementation of the co-creation journeys of the labs while focusing on a better understanding of the particularities within each context.

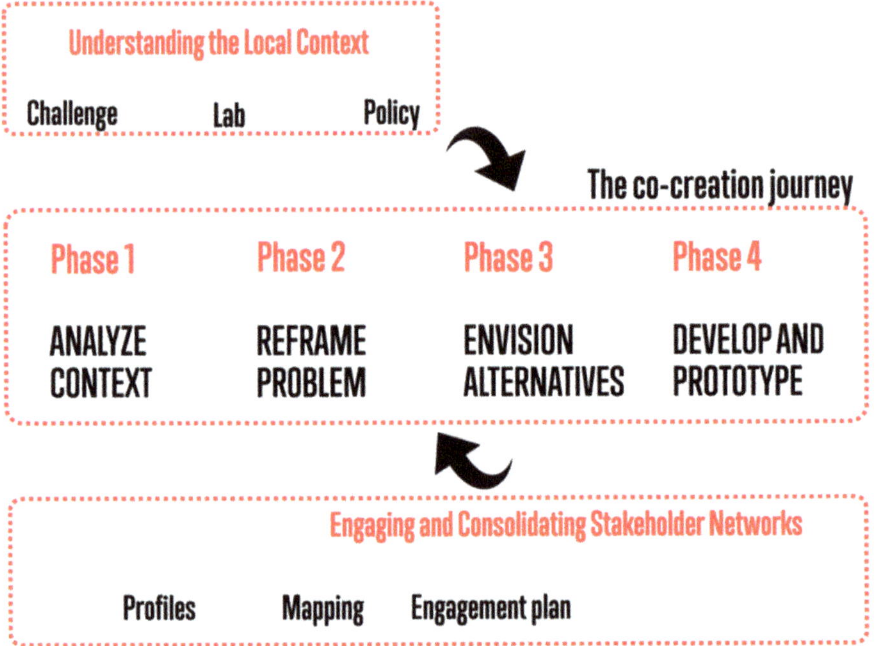

Fig. 2 Application process of the design-based learning framework

A premise to the construction of the toolbox is an extensive desk research aimed at analysing co-design in RRI in literature as well as investigating existing cases in Europe and beyond. The needs and gaps identified during this research led to the definition of a set of goals to be translated in specifications for development of the toolbox as pictured in Table 1. This toolbox was developed before the start of the experimentation, composed by a set of important instruments to use in an entirely flexible way throughout the co-creation journey. In the following, the main goals and their sub-goals are reported that were identified as key elements in the design process to be translated in specification that lead the construction of the toolbox (Fig. 3).

The learning framework and the toolbox as the two main aspects of the applied experimentation concept are meant to give a clear framework to the experimentation itself and support the process to reach the objectives stated in the following.

Table 1 Goals of the experimentation and resulting specifications for the toolbox

Goals	Details	Specifications for the toolbox design
Fill the identified RRI gaps	Complexity of societal problems	Context-based approach using systemic tools
	Engagement of stakeholders	Use of stakeholder canvases all along the journey
	Tangibility of RRI projects	Use of prototypes as boundary objects
Make the single tools modular and customisable	Context Matters	Adaptable selection of tools according to cases
	Tools appropriation	Support provided to enlarge the practical knowledge about tools. 101 methods design cards
Trigger reflexivity through the use of tools	Comparison necessities	Process characterised by common macro-phases that can be freely organised in sub-phases, and on the other hand the adoption of a limited set of common tools that synthesize the outcomes of each phase
	Common knowledge spaces	Organisation of interactive moments with partners like lab exchange day, skype call and communication spaces (social media, website…)

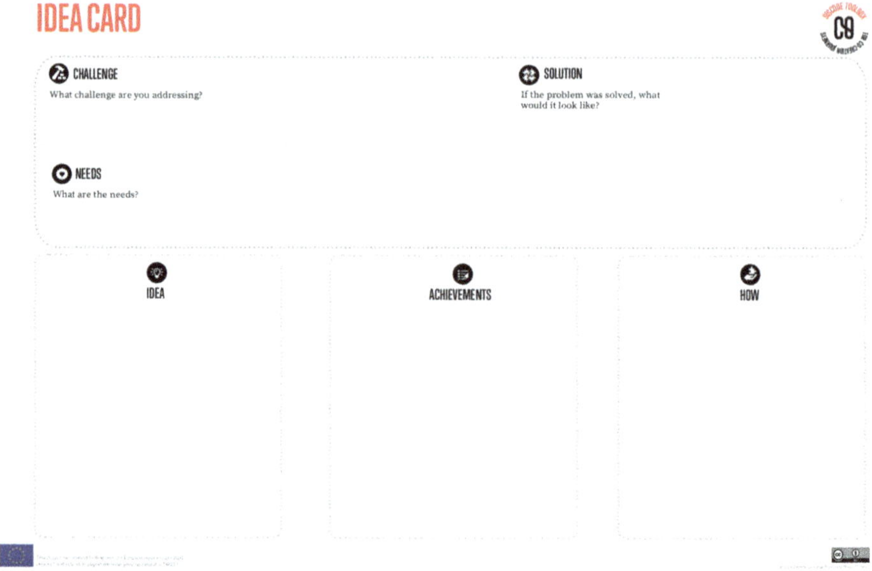

Fig. 3 Idea card—an example from the toolbox

3 Key Objectives and Originality of the Approach

As anticipated, each experimentation aims at the conduction of high-impact investigations in a real-life context. Through the direct engagement of a variety of users and actors in a process of action research as well as the tackling of a relevant societal challenge it aims to influence current organisational structures and policies at a wider scale. In this, the effectiveness of design methods is tested in an RRI context to move from sheer ideation to implementation.

Prototypes as a means to move from co-design to co-production
Having identified the issue to move from ideation to implementation [7], bridging this gap is one of the main objectives in the experimentation. The underlying assumption is that design methodologies and tools are suitable to support co-creation for the inclusion of society in science and innovation and exploit their practical orientation to bridge the aforementioned gap between ideation and implementation. What differentiates design from other co-creation methodologies is the role of prototypes and their experimentation in real contexts [8]. Prototypes can provide support in shortening the distance between "co-construction and its outcomes as they are refracted through practicalities embedded in existing institutions and interests" (SwafS-13-2017 topic) [9].

The experimentation of this potential in a real context is crucial to explore the possibilities of bridging the gap between ideal and real outputs that the application of co-creation and RRI can produce.

Prototyping all revolves around giving people the space and time to materialize and concretize their ideas, it brings an experience to a vision by creating objects of dialog and designs that can afford interaction with people and place, to evoke debate to capture the potential and risks involved in innovation.

Prototyping arouses empowerment, dialog, acts of creation and intents of empiricism and allows practitioners to connect with realities and representations when navigating towards the unknown.

Prototypes are objects manifesting the interconnection between ideas, matter, theory and practices, bringing together soft systems and Hard Technologies. In the approach, it is hypothesised they can create bridges between projects, scales and stakeholders to support innovation.

Implementing RRI

While the potential of RRI as a new approach has been widely discussed in theory, a lack of its translation into practice has been identified [7]. With its attitude of previously evaluating impacts on the entire ecosystem of operation and society RRI involves a variety of actors, including users and stakeholders, in the entire development process from the very beginning. The experimentation concretely explored the engagement of a variety of stakeholders using techniques and processes from the field of design to operationalise this element of RRI involving actors from an early stage keeping them engaged throughout the process.

Therefore, material is being produced to feed theoretical studies with experiences in practice and application in real life. Concretely, theoretical concepts found during the desk research on how RRI are experimented and verified for their implementability to undermine or confute the research statements from a practical point of view.

This new approach together with the active participation is also meant to provoke a learning process within the world of policymaking. The objective is to create a fertile ground where to show possibilities and functioning of different approaches opening up policymaking as a field that has been found to be often restricted and closed in itself creating a safe playground for policymakers to experiment further, acquire new knowledge and build themselves capacities in applying this knowledge.

Capacity building and organisational change through co-design

The objectives of capacity building within the pilots' ecosystem are twofold: On one hand, the capacity of co-creation within the lab leading the pilot is aimed to be enhanced through the training provided during the project and the frequent and iterative application and use of co-design tools. This knowledge generation on co-creation is planned to go beyond the members of the labs involved, extending beyond that to the application in other projects and to their spread over the entire organisation as a means to co-create and lead co-creation initiatives themselves. On the other hand, a further learning effect is meant to be provoked in the entire ecosystem, including all actors and stakeholders involved in the activities of the experimentation. In a learning-by-doing process their knowledge on the use of design methodologies and their capacities to cope with barriers and constraints that may occur in the process are expected to be built in consequence of practical activities. In this case, this means developing knowledge because of their involvement in the co-design and the prototyping of specific solutions.

To support and further exploit the bridges built between policymakers and practitioners as well to give other interested policymakers the tools and possibilities to experiment with new approaches, the best practices, learning outcomes and direct feedback from policymakers are to be analysed and used to produce an open repository of material, tools and instruction that have been proven successful in introducing design into policymaking to spread and disseminate precious evidences collected throughout the project.

4   The Networks and Labs

The cases of application of new processes and visions to involve actors that have not been considered in the development process of new initiatives to date are constantly growing. Greater, international networks function as a collector for those often smaller initiatives and labs to provide support and foster the exchange among different realities in local contexts and challenges to provide a broader view on small-scale experiments and reflect on interconnections, scalability and replicability in diverse contexts.

Description of networks and labs involved
The experimentation took place in 10 co-creation labs spread across Europe. All 10 labs are members of one of the three networks mentioned in the following.

The Fab City Foundation
The community of Fab Labs spreads over more than 78 countries with approximately 1000 members including fabricators, scientists, educators and professionals of labs of all sizes from community-based small labs to research centers. Their common goal is the democratization of access to the tools for technical inventions and the spread of the culture of making. They are also experimenting with new approaches and engagement of stakeholders to create new urban models within the Fab City initiative.

European Network of Living Labs (ENoLL)
The European Network of Living Labs with headquarter in brussels, Belgium is composed of more than 400 recognised Living Labs as environments for open innovation and promoting co-creation, stakeholder participation and active actor involvement in real contexts.

European Network of Science Centres and Museums (ECSITE)
Ecsite connects science communication professionals from more than 400 institutions located in 50 countries. It connects member institutions through projects and activities facilitating collaboration and the exchange of ideas and best practices on current issues. Their members engage citizens in science fostering creativity and critical thinking to inspire and empower society (Table 2).

Table 2 Overview of the labs taking part in the experimentation

Lab	Description
Maker *Copenhagen (Denmark)* *Fab Lab*	*Maker* is a non-profit association with the core objective of connecting and supporting communities of makers and their methodologies to the public and new sectors to facilitate new relationships and collaborations among makers, civil society, private and public organisations as well as policymakers
Fab Lab Barcelona *Barcelona (Spain)* *Fab Lab*	*Fab Lab Barcelona* is a part of the Institute for Advanced Architecture of Catalonia supporting a variety of education- and research programs related to the human habitat on different scales. Its mission is the provision of access to knowledge, tools and financial means to foster technology-based and digital innovation and invention for the improvement of life quality
Polifactory *Milan (Italy)* *Fab Lab*	*Polifactory* is the makerspace inside Politecnico Milano as a multidisciplinary research lab between design, mechanical engineering, electronics and bioengineering. By the promotion of a new culture of making new ways of manufacturing and production systems are explored including areas like research, experimental and peer-to-peer education and cultural dissemination
PA4ALL *Novi Sad (Serbia)* *Living Lab*	Applying a multidisciplinary approach, *PA4ALL*, part of the Biosense Institute, is focused on Precision Agriculture operating between the fields of ICT, Agriculture, Environmental Engineering and Ecology Involving multiple stakeholders *PA4ALL* combines user needs with technology and innovative methodologies bring together users, public institutions, researchers and technology
ThessAHALL *Thessaloniki (Greece)* *Living Lab*	The Thessaloniki Active and Healthy Ageing Living Lab (*Thess-AHALL*) is governed by the Laboratory of Medical Physics of the Aristotle University of Thessaloniki operating in real community settings with a wide network of collaborators in Greece and the Balkan region. Adopting co-creation approaches they enable user-driven innovation in the field of Activity & Health
KTP *Krakow (Poland)* *Living Lab*	The Krakow Technology Park is a key actor in the development and implementation of Regional Innovation Strategies promoting user-driven innovation and smart specialisation. With an ecosystem of 300 companies they support innovative technology-oriented businesses at different stages of development with a variety of services testing their products and services in a Living Lab environment involving end users and a variety of stakeholders

(continued)

Table 2 (continued)

Lab	Description
Cube design museum *Kerkrade* *(Netherlands)* *Science Centers & Museums*	*Cube design museum* is part of Stichting Museumplein Limburg, a foundation that tells the story of the earth, sustainability, science, technology and design, in the context of society and education Cube's exhibitions are dedicated to design for human needs and ambitions including a lab to co-create with the public to provide open access to design tools and enhance their use for society
TRACES *Paris (France)* *Science Centers & Museums*	As a non-profit association between participatory science engagement and social inclusion and a strong orientation towards innovation in research *TRACES* aims to create space for reflection, experimentation and innovation for science in society, science education and communication
Ciência Viva *Lisbon (Portugal)* *Science Centers & Museums*	The Portuguese agency for public awareness of science and technology is a non-profit association in the fields of science awareness, science education and open science. One of its main focus is on ocean literacy
SGD *Dublin (Ireland)* *Science Centers & Museums*	*Science Gallery Dublin (SGD)* is a living experiment by Trinity College Dublin to encourage young people in an encounter of art and science. Unique exhibitions that allow participation and social connections of visitors while exploring different aspects of one topic

5 Support and Assessment Procedures

During their co-creation journey, the labs have received support from the various project members and partners of SISCODE to fully exploit all present capacities to combine the knowledge and abilities of practitioners and research partners. Apart from active support to acquire knowledge on co-creation and its potential application during the co-creation journey a peer-to-peer learning among labs and other interested partners has been fostered to enhance exchange on experiences, practices, issues and identified opportunities not only to confront with other, similar realities, but also to self-reflect on current practices and how they could be improved in the future.

One of the main struggles that RRI is facing when moving from theory to practice is the assessment of its impact within the context on application. To tackle this in the specific project, an assessment framework has been set up to gather, mainly qualitative data, from the pilots during their journey to monitor and evaluate their progress. Initially planned to measure solely the success of the single pilots, the assessment framework soon turned into an instrument to measure impact on a greater level retrieving data on changes and transformations caused in the pilots' organisations and ecosystems beyond the single prototype.

The assessment explores three different dimensions to be explored specifically, namely the ones of:

1. **Stakeholder engagement**, previously named as a fundamental aspect of the entire project being both a crucial part of RRI and co-design identifying and involving a variety of actors
2. **Co-creation,** the means for operationalisation and the base for the methodology applied in the overall project investigating the effectiveness and appropriation of the techniques and tools used
3. **Dissemination**, the opportunity and capacity to share successes and failures, practice knowledge exchange and foster capacity building beyond the project's borders.

Three tools have been developed to assess the dimensions throughout the process:

- **Excel spreadsheet** focused on the reporting of activities conducted and numbers of actors involved to keep track of direct outputs in the process
- **Self-assessment questionnaire** a questionnaire exploring the outcomes on a broader dimensions and from a qualitative point of view triggering self-reflection on current practices in the organisation as well as organisational change
- **Scenarios** to illustrate possible near futures to create an outlook on how the pilot could impact the organisation and the ecosystem in the long-term.

The goal of the monitoring and assessment activity is the evaluation of the single cases applying the three tools described previously either in a continuous way throughout the experimentation like done with the spreadsheet or accurately at specific points of the journey.

Its results are not only meant to assess the single prototypes, but also allow a comparison among them and feed broader reflections on the application of co-creation in RRI contexts and its impact assessment that is elaborated in the final chapter of this book.

To allow this comparison and further evaluation of the cases, it has been decided to elaborate them singularly as case studies after the conclusion of the prototyping phase. The following chapter goes in detail on the choice of the methodology and the guidelines developed to guide and regulate the writing.

References

1. Rizzo F, Deserti A, Crabu S, Smallman M, Hjort J, Hansen SJ, Menichinelli M (2018) Co-creation in RRI practices and STI policies. SISCODE deliverable D1.2, https://ec.europa.eu/research/par ticipants/documents/downloadPublic?documentIds=080166e5bedc3a0d&appId=PPGMS, last accessed 2021/03/21
2. Jakobsen SE, Fløysand A, Overton J (2019) Expanding the field of responsible research and innovation (RRI)—from responsible research to responsible innovation. Eur Plan Stud 27:2329–2343
3. Deserti A, Eckhardt J, Kaletka C, Rizzo F, Vasche E (2019) Co-design for society in innovation. In: Atlas of social innovation, vol 2. Oekom, Munich, pp 91–96
4. Rizzo F, Deserti A, Komatsu TT (2020) Implementing Social Innovation in real contexts. Int J Knowl Based Dev 11(1):45–67

5. Blomkamp E (2018) The promise of co-design for public policy. Aust J Public Adm 77(4):729–743
6. Kolb DA (1983) Experiential learning: experience as the source of learning and development, 1 edn. Englewood Cliffs, NJ: Prentice Hall
7. Von Schomberg R (2013) A vision of responsible research and innovation. In: Responsible innovation: managing the responsible emergence of science and innovation in society, pp. 51–74
8. Rizzo F, Cantu D (2013) From designing in protected environment to designing in real contexts-Piloting digital services for elderly independent living. In: IASDR conference, International Association of Societies of Design Research, 2, pp 2585–2596
9. European Commission: Integrating Society in science and innovation—an approach to co-creation, https://ec.europa.eu/info/funding-tenders/opportunities/portal/screen/opportunities/topic-details/swafs-13-2017. Last accessed 2020/10/12

Framing Real-Life Experimentations as Case Studies

Stefano Crabu, Ilaria Mariani, and Felicitas Schmittinger

The chapter describes the case studies methodology on the ground of the volume: their use and comparison are investigated from a theoretical point of view. This chapter has a twofold aim: (i) contextualise case studies and the experimentation/prototyping conducted by the pilots, then (ii) to provide a compass for going through the next chapters in which it is detailed the experience of each pilot as a case study. This reasoning is a premise for understanding and situating the relevant points emerged in the larger picture of the RRI framework.

1   Introduction

This chapter has the purpose of presenting the overall methodological framework in which the volume is rooted. It is aim to discuss the case study approach adopted for orienting the production of self- and reflexive narrations about ten RLEs carried out by as many pilot organisations across Europe (Fab Labs, Living Labs and Science Centers and Museums) engaged in addressing relevant societal challenges entangled with various STI domains. In doing so, a meaningful methodological compass is provided for understanding the rationale and the structure of the next ten "empirical chapters". More in detail, the following chapters are consecrated to discuss each "pilot experimentation" as a case study, which allow to critically present, analyse and

S. Crabu (✉) · I. Mariani · F. Schmittinger
Department of Design, Politecnico di Milano, 20158 Milan, Italy
e-mail: stefano.crabu@polimi.it

I. Mariani
e-mail: ilaria1.mariani@polimi.it

F. Schmittinger
e-mail: felicitas.schmittinger@polimi.it

A. Deserti et al. (eds.), *Co-creation for Responsible Research and Innovation*,
Springer Series in Design and Innovation 15,
https://doi.org/10.1007/978-3-030-78733-2_3

assess the effectiveness of the adopted co-creation approaches, processes and tools (see Chap. 2). Thus this chapter serves as a methodological premise for clarifying how data from the ten RLEs, in the form of self-narrative case studies, has been gathered allowing: (i) a deeper understanding of the major dimensions at stake in co-creation practices within STI domains and; (ii) a comparative analysis of these major dimensions within the context of the RRI frame.

2 The Case Study Approach

As mentioned above, a methodological frame was adopted according to which each RLE has been framed as a case study. The heuristic power of the case study approach is well recognised in different fields, such as social research, design, law and policy, due to its potential for eliciting in-depth, multi-faceted explorations of complex issues in their real-life, naturalistic settings. According to Yin [1], a case study can be defined: "as an empirical inquiry that investigates a contemporary phenomenon within its real-life context; when the boundaries between phenomenon and context are not clearly evident; and in which multiple sources of evidence are used." In this sense, the case study approach is one of the most relevant research strategies to employ for producing an in-depth and thorough appreciation of an event or phenomenon of interest occurring within its natural real-life context. In research, the case study approach can be mobilised, for example, to describe in details patient-physician relationships within different hospitals and how the mutual consent is shaped; or how different practitioners in high-tech firms cooperate for developing an innovative technological solutions for monitoring the air quality; or again to investigate causal links and pathways emerging by the implementation of a new regulatory initiative, or a public service in a concerned geographical area. As a rule, a case study framework selects a small geographical area or a limited number of organisations, or social groups to be scrutinized. Thereby, the case study approach allows a researcher to closely examine data within a specific context. So, case studies enable exploration and investigation of both ongoing real-life processes by means of contingent analysis of specific settings of interactions, and how interactions and conditions under study can influence, and are influenced by the cultural, economic and political landscape.

3 Eliciting Experiential Knowledge on Co-creation in STI Policymaking

A case study approach was adopted with the aim to investigate real-life co-design and co-creation practices in STI as a way to (re)shape the missing links between strategic objectives (to make research and innovation more "responsible"), topics and communities (domains of science and technology, groups of stakeholders, citizens and society at large), and the activities on the ground (research and innovation). This approach allowed to generate data and information around the "how", "what" and "why" questions at different levels (i.e. national, regional and local), and about different dimensions (i.e. economic, political and social). For example, it opens up reasonings about questions such as "how pre-existing culture of engagement and dialogue between citizens and stakeholders influenced the experimentation". This can support both in developing and refining fresh knowledge about the current forms of public participation in STI policymaking and beyond, as expected within the RRI frame. However, it is worth noticing that a case study is not aimed at exploring an entire organisation. Rather, the analytical gaze focalised on particular issues, by framing the specific RLE as the unit of analysis. This approach allows to understand the complexity of the RLE, by carefully designing and implementing what was called "the self-narration guidelines' (see Sect. 4). This tool enables the production and consistent organisation of the experiential knowledge shaped by the different kinds of practitioners engaged within the concerned RLE, e.g. designers, science communicators, engineers, students, patients and lay people in general. By means of the self-narration guidelines it was aimed at generating "thick description" [2] of what is going on within the experimentation. This work can be considered primarily as an observation activity of ordinary practice occurring in a specific setting. More critically, it is a reflexive activity oriented at producing a thorough account about the multiverse co-creation activities, thus to make sense of local meaning and local knowledge, and relating them to the broader organisational, social, political and economic context. This is provided by the fact that this self-narration casework is based on the direct participation of the authors in the real-time experimentation, spending extended time on site, personally organising co-creation activities of the case, reflecting and revising the descriptions of what is going on. Therefore, it is an analytical and reflexive effort aimed at understanding what is important about the specific experimentation within its own environment, which is peculiar and different for each case. The goal set by the self-narration guidelines is not to describe data as they occur during the RLEs; but to produce a detailed emic account able to provide actionable and analytical insights about how the co-creation experimentation took place, in its different phases, such as the definition of the challenge to be addressed and the process of designing the solutions.

As it will clearly emerge in the next section, in designing the self-narration guidelines specific attention was paid to the mutual engagement between the situated and specific practices for conduction the RLE, and the broad economic, political and social contexts. As a consequence, practitioners were asked to clarify regulatory landscapes and social values and beliefs that entered as a relevant dimension in the course of the experimentation. It is worth noticing that this strategy engendered complex relationships. Indeed, the self-narration guidelines pull attention both to the situated ordinary practices and experience of the practitioners and stakeholders engaged in the RLE and also to the broad large socio-political and regulatory contexts in which each experimentation is located. In this way, self-narration orients to complexities connecting ordinary practices of co-creation occurring in specific settings of interaction to some more broad concerns related to the regulatory and societal environments.

Thus, in this approach the *self-narration guidelines* enabled the consideration of the case study both as a process of learning about the specific RLT and the product of the learning produced in SISCODE. Under the aegis of this methodological approach firstly the RLEs are considered as a bounded system that allows to capture specificities at stake in STI co-creation around certain societal challenges developed according to the RRI. Furthermore, the self-narration guidelines work as an "instrumental case study", aimed at highlighting the specific methodological choices, the tools mobilised in the experimentation, and its interpretations in relation to the specific context in which the RTE has been performed.

Finally, in the last chapter the 10 case studies will be analysed as a whole, or as a "collective case study" [3] in order to develop a comparative investigation that can lead to a better understanding of co-creation processes in relation to the STI policymaking. This strategy offers an in-depth and comprehensive understanding of co-creation in Europe, and across different STI domains (such as health, ICT and environmental issues) as a bottom-up and design-led phenomenon together with its corresponding suitable framework conditions. In this way it is aimed to analyse and compare the outcome and condition of the RLEs under scrutiny, thus to assess the result of the impact of co-creation in STI policymaking in relation to the RRI frame. In doing so, the results of the comparative analysis (Chap. 14) will provide insights on suitable strategies for coping with the limit of the current implementation of co-creation in STI policy. Therefore, the comparative analysis is carried out according to the following dimensions:

i.   phases of the engagement process they support (i.e. research, Conceptualisation, development, prototyping and testing, assessment);
ii. expected output (i.e. opinions, feedbacks, ideas, product, and service);
iii. sectors of application (i.e. private, public, and third sector);
iv. typology of innovation (i.e. technological, social, scientific, and business).

Overall, innovative knowledge is offered on what works and what does not work to boost the operationalisation of RRI through co-creation.

4   The Self-narration Guidelines: Rationale and Layout

The reasoning that follows stems from the awareness that the RRI field reports a general lack of a learning framework aimed at supporting the validation and replication of virtuous mechanisms of co-creation for RRI. In such a context, gaining understanding on how to cope with constraints and barriers that frequently come about along the process constitutes relevant knowledge that can contribute to the successful result of other initiatives.

As stated in the previous paragraph, the basic concept of creating guidelines is based both on the concept of having the participants of the RLE themselves narrating the cases, as well as aligning different pilots in terms of typology of organisation, domains and addressed challenge, thus to make them comparable to some extent.

Moreover, introducing a unique format shared among the actors engaged in the RLEs paves the way for mutual understanding, contributing in building useful knowledge and consistent narrations about the processes of experimenting.

Exploiting their extensive knowledge of the process, the guidelines are meant to encourage those who compile them—namely the team involved in the co-creation within the labs—to describe their experience as a case considering all fundamental aspects while self-reflecting during the writing.

Given these premises, the objective of asking the team of each RLEs to represent their experimentation through the practice of self-narrations built upon the same guidelines is twofold.

At first, the pilots should have the possibility to narrate their co-creation journey themselves as protagonists of the process, without too much influence of third parties but providing a direction on the desired outcome. This has not only the scope to create a purely first-hand report from the people being directly involved in the experimentation, but also stimulate self-reflection during the writing activity itself. As a matter of fact, the reflective activity is valued that reaches across the process of writing as a moment of fundamental learning per se. On the other hand, providing guidelines as a general layout with key points and questions as an orientation is a way for aligning the very diverse pilots in a similar form, making their process and experiences to some extent comparable to each other. Notwithstanding their diverse background and context, and the fact that each lab focused on different challenges/experimentations, providing them with the same basic structure to follow was key for opening up comparison and critical analysis, nurturing a discussion that goes beyond the singular cases.

Therefore, the guidelines are the result of a methodological process applied to gather information on some aspects fundamental for the experimentation.

In the following the layout is reported as an index, anticipating that each part will be laid out later on sharing the rationale on their ground.

1. Synthesis of the pilot's journey.
2. Initial context.

  2.1. External context and ecosystem.
  2.2. Organisational background.

3. Challenge.
4. The co-creation process of the envisioned solution.

  4.1. Context analysis.
  4.2. Problem framing.
  4.3. Envisioning solutions.
  4.4. Developing and prototyping.
  4.5. The role of policies and policymaker engagement.

5. The Final Solution.

  5.1. Final concept.

5.2. Sustainability strategy.

6. Transformations triggered and outcomes.
7. Conclusive reflections.
8. References.

In addition to this index as a basic guideline, every section unpacks into key points referring to the desired content and contains a few questions aimed at triggering a detailed and in-depth description of the experimentation, while further stimulating reflection during the writing.

For example, in the final chapter on conclusive reflections, one of the questions had been "Did you come across some unexpected opportunities that you weren't aware of?" to invite the pilots to a broader reflection on alternatives and opportunities identified during the process.

The logic of the layout roughly follows the general co-creation journey that each lab underwent during the experimentation process (see Chap. 2), hence starting from the analysis of the context to the phase of developing and prototyping of the solution. As previously mentioned, the layout is directed towards the collection of specific information related to the main dimensions explored, namely the implementation of RRI in practice, the exploration of capacity building through co-design and prototyping as an approach to transform ideas into implementable solutions. Such dimensions and their enquiry were also carefully inspected during the desk research conducted in the first year of the SISCODE project, and consisting in an extensive literature review and an analysis of existing co-creation cases across Europe (n:138). This preliminary study grasped the potential of co-creation approaches, RRI practices and policies, and their cross-fertilisation to inform the experimentation on the dynamics and outcomes that spurred form of integrating society in science and innovation in a long-term perspective.

As a matter of fact, while RLEs benefited from the investigation of the state of the art regarding practices on co-creation in contexts, as well as from the knowledge base generated in such an enquiry to enrich their processes [4–6], the hereby presented guidelines leaned on such scholarship for defining the dimensions to specifically vet through its self-narrative approach.

Considering the overall objective of delivering insights into the use of collaborative approaches for RRI and policymaking, the analysis of RLEs as case studies needs to keep in mind that a successful implementation of co-creation strongly depends on the interaction with the context [7]. Such interaction has a high degree of complexity, since it is characterised by multilayered social dimensions on various levels. Grasping its logics is primary for a more precise understanding of the dynamics triggered in the ecosystem, as well as their opportunities and barriers [8, 9]. These can be attributed to three levels related to as many scales. The macro-level identifies a "process of change in the social structure of a society in its constitutive institutions, cultural patterns, associated social actions and conscious awareness" [10]. The meso-level refers to the intermediate structures as interactions with organisations and alliances. Finally, the micro-level covers the individual scale of the person, its needs and role-conflicts, and it allows to understand "how stakeholders and their everyday practices interact with environmental factors" [4].

To gain such an accurate knowledge, the guidelines pose specific attention to the exploration of the context of dependency, the way in which stakeholders are involved, the co-creation practices operated, and the transformations triggered, from the dimension of the team to at an organisational scale.

Table 1 unpacks the question starting from the overall goals of the experimentation, to their sub-elements, up to the link to the dimensions explored.

Context dependency

Context and its specificities constitute a structural factor to consider when dealing with co-creation and RRI, since it reflects established cultures, mindsets, practices, and policies characterising the specific environment [11]. Since co-creation practices take place in contexts as ecosystems that contain actors with their specificities and inter-dependencies, their understanding can highly impact the success of an initiative. Therefore, introducing this dimension is a way for asking labs to describe and reflect on the context where the experimentation is taking place. Taking this into high consideration means gaining understanding about the networks and partnerships the initiating body upholds, as well as about local culture, structures and policies. As its importance is meant to instruct the self-narrative of the labs, so it also exert its influence in terms of tools. When creating the toolbox (see Chap. 2), the recognised presence of extremely diverse contexts led to the need for modular and customisable tools and activities. The inherent heterogeneity and diversification of contexts had been identified as one of the barriers to the implementation of RRI. In consequence,

Table 1 Overall goals of the experimentation, sub-elements, and dimensions explored

Goals of the experimentation	Details	Dimension explored in case studies
Fill the identified RRI gaps	Complexity of societal problems	Context dependency
	Engagement of stakeholders	Context dependency Stakeholder involvement Co-creation practices
	Tangibility of RRI projects	Context dependency Stakeholder involvement Co-creation practices
Make the single tools modular and customisable & test their functionality	Context matters	Context dependency
	Tools appropriation	Context dependency Co-creation practices Capacity building and organisational change
Trigger reflexivity through the use of tools	Comparison necessities	Context dependency
	Common knowledge spaces	Co-creation practices Capacity building and organisational change

several tools were inserted in the toolbox aiming at encouraging to explore the influence of this dimension, valuing the surrounding context specifically relevant and its investigation in the policy context. In parallel, specific attention is drawn on how tools and methodologies are adopted individually by each lab in relation to the environment, as well as differences and similarities in regard to barriers and opportunities identified in diverse contexts.

Stakeholder involvement

The engagement and constant relationship with concerned actors is crucial both in co-design and RRI. Considering the relationship between the context where the problem is situated and the network that will co-create the solution is central [12–14]. Especially in co-creation processes, the interaction between people with different cultures, backgrounds and forms of knowledge within a frame of collaboration enables the opportunity for both conflict and a learning process where knowledge is shared among peers. Knowledge and expertise lies among different stakeholders, and their involvement enables them to grasp complementary and critical insights. Therefore, it becomes fundamental to identify the various stakeholders groups and local actors to be actively involved throughout the entire process. Being it simple user experience, social knowledge or 'expert' technical knowledge, the benefits from engaging the public goes beyond the verification of hypothesis. Relevant advice, then, regards the possibility to extract both behavioral schemes and best practices from their various domains of knowledge. Public participation is a way to recognise and value their motivation, needs and behaviors, as well as a way to develop context-based solutions [7].

Moreover, recognising that policymakers often do not value social knowledge as equal or valuable as 'expert' technical knowledge [7], the experimentation specifically focused on the inclusion of this group of stakeholders. Investigating possible interplays and interactions by involving policymakers along the entire co-creation becomes a way to better frame the context of STI policymaking in particular as one of the core objectives of the study.

Specific aspects to be explored in the analysis are the level of engagement (active or passive), the constancy throughout the various phases and their overall role.

Co-creation practices

Co-creation as the way to operationalise RRI in this experimentation is inspected under various aspects. On one hand, its general efficiency and efficacy in RRI contexts is to be explored together with the potential need to be adapted and modified to entirely satisfy the needs for its application in an RRI context.

Aspects to consider in this dimension are its changeableness and potential to be modified for specific contexts and situations, and how this variability can be communicated minimizing the risk of being too broad and open hindering the actual adoption. Finding this balance is specifically important for an effective introduction of co-creation. Here it is particularly relevant to reason about the risks that come across skepticism and resistance, especially in fields with very different current practices like policymaking. Ways to deal with this resistance are to be investigated as well.

Addressing how such aspects have been tackled by going through a process of self-narration is a way to encourage labs to gain further awareness about their learning, turning them into shareable knowledge.

Particular attention is drawn to the phase of prototyping as the transition from sheer ideas to potential implementable solutions [15]. This is a particularly crucial point to be investigated to evaluate the potential of the design approach to bridge the gap identified in RRI of moving towards real implementation [16].

Capacity building and organisational change

Co-creation can bring knowledge and assumptions about who contributes in creating solutions and defining policies, also challenging existing or established practices [7]. To ensure a long-term change and a full embedding of the design approach, the capacities related to it need to be fully incorporated into the organisation and its members to be applied successfully and trigger substantial change in the organisation [17].

The specific focus here lies on two kinds of knowledge acquisition. On one hand the capacities built within the organisation and their influence on its culture and practices beyond the project. On the other hand, the capacities acquired by participants that are not members of the organisation like stakeholders or users are investigated. This is relevant to explore the possibilities and methodologies of triggering change in external entities and actors through concrete involvement in a project. In fact, since they introduce practices and tools able to challenge an established order, co-creation and co-design are political acts. In consequence, it is paramount to invite labs to ruminate about the transformations they activated during their co-creation processes, especially focusing on aspects and situations that encountered resistance to change reflecting on potential futures and an outlook on long-term change.

Moreover, this dimension is also meant to encourage reflection about capacities developed along the way, as well as about barriers to capacity building encountered.

5 Implementing the Guidelines: 10 Experiences of Co-creation

Examples of realities where new visions and processes of co-design aimed at actively involving stakeholders in the co-creation of solutions and favourable policies and frameworks are flourishing across Europe in innovation labs exploring citizen science like policy labs, Living Labs, Fab Labs or Science Centers and Museums. Within this context, the experimentation has been implemented in three main domains, that of Fab Labs (n:3), Living Labs (n:3), and Science Centres and Museums (n:4).

Recognising that the range of practices depends on the several variables of the complex landscape where co-creation and design take place, innovation labs come to the fore for being spaces where design-led practices are translated into implementable solutions. In particular, they emerge as characterised by a variety of approaches and tools not only adopted but often further developed to meet their needs and better answer to local conditions and challenges, showing an inherent openness to experimentation while being adaptive and flexible.

In the following chapters it will be explored how the structured process of self-narration intended for connecting the practice with the capacity to set up an analytical, reflective and learning framework, encouraged to frame and make the experiential knowledge gathered intelligible. Although they all aim at a better inclusion and participation of society in science, technology and innovation, each experiment presents its own challenge, context, features and peculiarities, as demonstrated and discussed in the following chapters.

References

1. Yin RK (1984) Case study research: design and methods. Sage, Beverly Hills, CA
2. Geertz C (1973) The interpretation of cultures: selected essays. Basic Books, New York, NY
3. Stake RE (1994) Qualitative case studies. In: Denzin NK, Lincoln L (eds) Handbook of qualitative research. Sage, London, pp. 443–466
4. Eckhardt J, Kaletka C, Klimek T (2019) SISCODE knowledge base. SISCODE deliverable D2.1, https://ec.europa.eu/research/participants/documents/downloadPublic?documentIds=080166e5c1fca367&appId=PPGMS, last accessed 2021/01/21
5. Kaletka C, Eckhardt J, Krüger D (2018) Theoretical framework and tools for understanding co-creation in contexts. SISCODE deliverable D1.3. https://ec.europa.eu/research/participants/documents/downloadPublic?documentIds=080166e5bed185fb&appId=PPGMS. Last accessed 2021/01/21
6. Smallman M, Patel T (2018) RRI research landscape. SISCODE deliverable D1.1. https://ec.europa.eu/research/participants/documents/downloadPublic?documentIds=080166e5bed17e30&appId=PPGMS. Last accessed 2021/03/02
7. Rizzo F, Deserti A, Crabu S, Smallman M, Hjort J, Hansen SJ, Menichinelli M (2018) Co-creation in RRI practices and STI policies SISCODE deliverable D1.2. https://ec.europa.eu/research/participants/documents/downloadPublic?documentIds=080166e5bedc3a0d&appId=PPGMS. Last accessed 2020/11/21
8. Domanski D, Howaldt J, Kaletka C (2020) A comprehensive concept of social innovation and its implications for the local context—on the growing importance of social innovation ecosystems and infrastructures. Eur Plan Stud 28:454–474
9. Kaletka C, Markmann M, Pelka B (2017) Peeling the onion. An exploration of the layers of social innovation ecosystems. Modelling a context sensitive perspective on driving and hindering factors for social innovation. Eur Public Soc Innov Rev 1(2)
10. Zapf W (2003) Sozialer Wandel. In: Schäfers B (ed) Grundbegriffe der Soziologie. Leske + Budrich, Opladen, pp 427–433
11. Howaldt J, Schwarz M (2010) Social innovation: concepts, research fields and international trends. Sozialforschungsstelle, Dortmund
12. Deserti A, Rizzo F (2014) Design and organisational change in the public sector. Des Manag J 9:85–97
13. Deserti A, Rizzo F (2020) Context dependency of social innovation: in search of new sustainability models. Eur Plan Stud 28:864–880
14. Manzini E, Rizzo F (2011) Small projects/large changes: participatory design as an open participated process. CoDesign 7:199–215
15. Blomkvist J, Holmlid S (2011) Existing prototyping perspectives: considerations for service design. Nordes 4
16. von Schomberg R (2013) A vision of responsible research and innovation. In: Owen R, Bessant J, Heintz M (eds) Responsible innovation. Wiley, Chichester, pp 51–74

17. Junginger S, Sangiorgi D (2009) Service design and organisational change. Bridging the gap between rigour and relevance. In: International association of societies of design research. KOR, pp 4339–4348

FabLab Barcelona—Co-design With Food Surplus: Better Redistributing, Upcycling and Composting

Marion Real, Anastasia Pistofidou, and Milena Juarez Calvos

The chapter analyses a co-designed project in the food value chain. Looking at how to identify and stimulate new synergies among the local community in order to co-develop educational, logistic and environmental supports for better redistributing, upcycling and composting food locally, it critically presents the case of a symbiotic system for food surplus and bio waste valorisation at a neighbourhood scale.

1 Introduction

IAAC\Fab Lab Barcelona is renowned as a key educational organisation in the Fab Lab Network since 2007 participating in the strategy and coordination of programs involving more than 1800 Fab Labs worldwide. *IAAC\Fab Lab Barcelona* is promoting innovation for sharing and circular cities with a focus on education, community empowerment and seven strategic areas of expertise: Sense Making, Productive Cities, Materials and Textiles, Future Learning, Civic Ecology, Distributed Design, and Emergent Futures. They have a pioneering and original approach of co-creation at the crossroad between peer learning, citizen science [29], digital fabrication and distributed design, central to engage with local communities.

M. Real (✉) · A. Pistofidou · M. Juarez Calvos
IAAC, Fab Lab Barcelona, Barcelona, Spain
e-mail: marion@fablabbcn.org

A. Pistofidou
e-mail: anastasia@fablabbcn.org

M. Juarez Calvos
e-mail: milena@fablabbcn.org

© The Author(s) 2022

A. Deserti et al. (eds.), *Co-creation for Responsible Research and Innovation,*
Springer Series in Design and Innovation 15,
https://doi.org/10.1007/978-3-030-78733-2_4

This practice has been built along the years thanks to European projects especially like Making Sense,[1] DDMP,[2] ISCAPE[3] [6, 14, 16].

The co-creation journey in SISCODE started with the wish of creating a playground for atterizing the Fab City vision [5] into the locality of Barcelona, in the creative neighbourhood of Poblenou. Since 2019, the team explored how makerspaces such as fablabs can foster local transformations guided by circular community and distributed manufacturing principles. After a first contextual analysis, the local team could emphasise the importance of food and plastic waste in Catalunya and discover new design practices emerging from new bioeconomy trends [8]. They opted to address the issue of food waste creating synergies with the maker ecosystem, food stakeholders and organisations of civil society in the area.

Cycles of collective activities, individual coaching and access to infrastructure were proposed by the lab to support an emergent community group to learn, nest and co-produce new design practices with food waste. Named Remix El Barrio, is now defined as *a collective of designers who propose projects with food leftovers using artisan techniques and digital manufacturing to foster circular transformations in Poblenou.*

2 Ecosystem, Context and Challenge Addressed

Catalonia region and the city of Barcelona are the cradle of the Fab City network and many innovative practices related to bottom-up approaches, participative policy design processes and citizen-led platform like SmartCitizen, SuperBarrio and DECIDIM[4] [4]. As many cities and regions, they have also initiated the development of circular economy action plans [18]. The climate action (from 2018 to 2030) is highlighting actions for responsible consumption, zero waste and food sovereignty and dedicating a specific part for the design of new training programs in the circular economy [2]. Beyond that, they have been really active in the food-chain value transformation especially with the program of the World Capital of Sustainable Food 2021. Concerning food waste, an important and innovative law [1] has been signed in 2020 and a dynamic network of stakeholders is now operationalising the strategy with promising changes to accelerate a better valorisation of food cycles in territories.

When zooming in the territorial distribution, the crucial role played by the neighborhoods (aka barrio) in reconnecting people's intentions and communities to public institutions becomes visible [15]. The city originally introduced a plan for creating self-sufficient neighbourhoods and relevant solutions to empower citizens and face social struggles.

---

[1] http://making-sense.eu/.

[2] https://distributeddesign.eu/.

[3] https://iscapeproject.eu/.

[4] https://www.decidim.barcelona/ and http://superbarrio.iaac.net/.

Poblenou is one of the neighbourhoods situated in the Sant Marti district, an old industrial area in urban regeneration since 17 years, Poblenou is now a mixed place that joins the old and the new, hosts many creative designers and innovative companies while fostering a large ecosystem of cooperatives and social enterprises, an interesting and complex playground for prototyping with the Fab City framework and move towards circular and bioeconomy transitions.

Challenge

The rise of material flows due to linear supply chain models is critical in urban context. Plastic production and related pollution are no longer viable for sustaining the biodiversity while food waste represents one third of the food present in the supply chain [13]. Waste Management strategies, circular initiatives and new design practices for reducing or designing with food waste are recently seen as great opportunities to better close the loop of systems and create materials from alternative sources that potentially reduce the environmental impact of more conventional materials. This will depend on the fabrication processes and local realities of production and uses. Thus, there is an interest in developing local communities that explore and sustain this new form of craft (neocraft) and manufacturing in a co-creative and responsible way.

The SISCODE journey of *IAAC|Fab Lab Barcelona* explores the following challenge with an intervention in the neighborhood of Poblenou:

How could co-creation foster the development of innovative ecosystems by crafting and micro-fabricating with food surplus and waste?

3 The Co-creation Journey

Context analysis

The journey started by analysing the local context and identifying the policies and local ecosystem relating to circular economy, social innovation and urban development. After conducting desk research, participating in 5 public events, conducting 35 interviews, the team gathered a common base of knowledge and future interventions. This preliminary grounding resulted in three outputs: an illustrated timeline of initiative's interviewees, a patchwork of the neighbourhood diversity and a stakeholder mapping based on different models of food value chains and food waste hierarchies.

Problem framing

To better frame the challenge, the local team has organised an original event to share the first bases of knowledge to a real group of stakeholders of the neighborhood and focus on the effective needs and motivations highlighted by thems. In this first co-creation workshop named "Synergy Soup" ("Sopa de Sinergias"), invited stakeholders took part in creative activities while preparing and eating a soup made with local collected food ingredients. The organisers could collect and discuss 58 needs,

36 resources and 31 ideas of projects. An interactive categorization of ideas were proposed in an open exhibition in IAAC (The Open Day of Poblenou) where visitors could discover and classify each idea in a matrix that allowed to show and draw how to locally improve material and food cycles at the neighbourhood scale. As a result of those activities, a first group of stakeholders engaged in the co-creation project with five categories of concepts to explore deeper: how to create a collective bank for vegetable seeds and design a Fab Yurt (a mini Fab Lab designed in and for an urban garden)? How to support the local collection of recovered food? How to design with bio-based materials? How to build a library of things? How to promote collective composting?

Envisioning solutions

To better envision the future solutions while keeping on rising community engagement, the team has organised a series of five 3-h-events that took place in different places of the neighborhood, between the 28th May and 28th June 2019 and that were communicating in a same flyer diffused both online and off-line in restaurants and community places:"¡Haz Comunidad!" (28.05.19), Practicing making (8.06. + 11.06.19), Eco-design and future narratives (18.06.19), convivial agora (28.06.2019).

Those events ranged from ideation sessions with customised tools (like 6Ws, backcasting value opportunity mapping, idea cards, eco-design and scenario building convivial design methods) to learning-by-doing experiences on digital fabrication tools and biomaterial design.

The participants had the opportunities to refine concept proposals, network with other stakeholders and get introduced crafting new materials using different processes.

The events strenghtened connections and enabled the rise of a local symbiotic system model representing each stakeholder with food waste project solutions at the neighbourhood scale. Fructifying from the discussions, the core team could integrate a layer of community services needed to support the development of such systems, consisting in new infrastructures for synergy stimulation, shared learning and design, production and logistics.

The workshop on biomaterial organized by Fabtextiles and based on past researches from the Fabricademy network and aimed at exploring the potential of material innovation from food waste raised a particular attention among the stakeholders that clearly demonstrate an interest in exploring further techniques and social experiences to scale it at the neighborhood scale.

Developing and prototyping

The prototyping phase started after a reflective summer and a creative phase of planning where the team could publish their initial model and participate in various local events to reconnect with the community members. The governance of the pilot and local team were revised to adjust the new needs for co-production, creating operational internal teams and a more strategic committee at Poblenou's scale.

The prototyping phase went into two main iterations. The first loop was composed of three fuzzy explorative projects: the co-design of a cargo bike km0, the exploration of products based from locally collected eggshells and an awareness campaign endorsing food waste valorisation initiatives. All projects ran in parallel and ended with an open event to showcase the results and ideate on future actions.

In the second loop, the team co-developed and facilitated an incubation programme about circular systems from food waste and surplus. Through an open cal for ideas, the extended co-creation team selected 13 projects, and invited them to start the incubation programme and engage through an agreement with the Fab Lab offering material provision, access to infrastructure, a shared online access, weekly collective session and individual coaching.

With the pandemic context, the program has been extended. It was beneficial both for the team and the participants who could reinforce their cooperation, better finalise their projects and go deeper in the definition of contents and external interventions. It allowed the creation of a series of online events "Remix in conversation", the implementation of individual feedback assessment. The programme ended with a final intervention: the co-design of an exhibition aiming at showcasing their projects and campaign in the barrio to activate new bonds and more awareness about food-waste-material making. More than 400 people, from newbies to gurus of design, from neighbors to policymakers visited the exhibition which took place in the Leka restaurant [26] following the barrier gestures and necessary restrictions imposed by COVID-19.

The role of policies and policymaker engagement
Since its initiation 17 years prior, IAAC has collaborated with a wide scope of strategic policy partners in the fields of urbanisation, computerised economy, culture and schooling. Barcelona City Council worked intimately with IAAC and *Fab Lab Barcelona* through numerous projects to advance new models of development, uphold the maker district backing the Fab City agenda. They worked on the project mode, collaborating according to circonstances and necessities. IAAC does not use formalised methodologies or approaches for connecting with policymakers. Internal dialogs remind primordial to initiate and sustain contacts with policymakers. In the SISCODE pilot, it is impossible to say that they effectively take part actively in the daily co-creation activities, however they had impacted the process or encouraged the team. The team realised that the presence or absence of policymakers associated as direct partners in such co-creation projects has a direct influence on their involvement.

Facing the difficulties to directly engage them in co-creation activities, IAAC team used more indirect strategies to reach them and benefit from their feedback and support. Here the most impactful ones:

- Conducting informal interviews with civil servants in the early stage of the process
- Be aware and active in local political events
- Create a climate of mutual trust to facilitate direct logistics and communication
- Co-organising activities and events led by the city (beyond the label of service providers)
- Applying for city funding and local communication calls.

Finally, the team has created a policy brief at the end of the project in the format of a manifiesto to communicate the recommendations of the collective Remix El Barrio for the design of future policies on scaling circular ecosystem crafting and micro-fabricating with food waste. This document has been transmitted to local and european stakeholders via direct mailing, catalogue online diffusion and diffusion in social media.

4 Experimentation: Output, Transformations, Outcomes

Remix El Barrio is now a collective of designers who propose projects with food leftovers using artisan techniques and digital manufacturing. They collaborate with agents from the Poblenou neighborhood to foster a more local and circular ecosystem. 9 main projects were developed: Kofi developed proposed to make paper and packaging from coffee waste; Naifactory and En(des)uso is creating lamps, chairs and pots from olive pits, eggshells, mate; Squeeze the Orange has designed an entire jacket made with orange peels; Colores is creating natural dyeing from avocado pits; Dulce de Piel is designing soap from used oils; Look Ma No Hand and Circular Gos are cooking snacks respectively for neighbors and dogs from restaurant leftovers.

Remix El Barrio is more than the sum of individual projects mentorised by the Fab Lab. Members are united around the values of local cooperation, solidarity, new form of crafts and circularity in Barcelona. They are supporting each other, campaigning together and co-producing a set of new experiences.

Beyond two research publications [19, 22], three main outputs were recently co-created: the design of exhibitions and its catalogues in two languages,[5] the development of video tutorials[6] and the co-elaboration of Gitbook[7] [3, 23, 24]. The initiative were awarded as Grand Prize for Innovative Collaboration by the Starts Prize 2021 [28].

The exhibition "Remix El Barrio—Co-design of biomaterials from food leftovers in Poblenou" first took place from 14.10.2019 to 23.10.2020 in the open source Restaurant LEKA [26]. It contains the nine projects accompanied by other artefacts of the SISCODE co-creation journey, a special creation from the Fabricademy, locally crafted labels and posters. The exhibition benefit from the visibility of the Fab City Summit,[8] the Poblenou Urban District open day/night,[9] the Foodture event[10] and the local FOOD SHIFT pilot kick-off[11] [7, 11, 12, 20]. The exhibition has been

---

[5] https://issuu.com/iaac/docs/remix_el_barrio_catalogo_en__1__compressed.

[6] https://www.youtube.com/playlist?list=PL33KKs9g8Y1K4MJGAUHpMZn-wMcbOVhnV.

[7] https://flbcn.gitbook.io/remix-el-barrio/.

[8] https://fablabbcn.org/calendar/fabcitysummit2020.

[9] https://www.poblenouurbandistrict.com/es/category/poblenou-urban-district/podn12h/.

[10] http://www.foodture.barcelona/.

[11] https://foodshift2030.eu/labs/food-tech-3-0-lab/.

replicated from March to May 2021 in the design hub of Barcelona in collaboration with Materfad [17] and the attendance of more 1000 visitors.

In times of COVID-19, online tutorials appeared as a relevant media to transmit practical hands-on knowledge. *Fab Lab Barcelona* Communication's team has collaborated with the team of Remix El Barrio to shoot and edit a set of 9 trial videos reviewing biomaterial recipes step by step from preparation, cooking and use.

The book describes the narratives of the co-creation journey, presents the 9 key design projects and associated educational materials such as a map of interactions with business models and emergent future stories, presents a list of tips, tools, recipes, courses, and protocols to better develop educational and incubation programs.

The team of *IAAC\Fab Lab Barcelona* experienced new learnings on co-creation and became more familiar with the respective processes and competences needed to apply it in a more structured way for long term projects. The co-creation lab has made explicit and challenged ongoing practices about stakeholder engagement, design processes, lab management, communication, policy context analysis.

Internally, the co-creation lab has contributed to the structuration of a circular community expertise and the creation of knowledge crossing the strategic areas of productive cities and Material and Textiles. It occured at the same time that many organisational changes in *Fab Lab Barcelona*. The core team members could learn about the agile environment and benefit of time to reflect on those practices dialoguing with SISCODE partners.

In terms of stakeholder engagement, it can be said that Remix El Barrio engaged with a dense network of stakeholders from local to global community. It is interesting to highlight the position of the lab as an interface between the members of the collective, the local community partners and the distributed networks, allowing synergy making, knowledge and technological infrastructure sharing and project incubation. The stakeholder management process is echoing with ongoing models and practices developed within the distributed design communities while really giving value to the importance of "real-time" situated supports, interaction and attitudes.

Beyond SISCODE, the team is now offering a panel of approaches not only to integrate circular principles and projects in existing global Fab Lab academies, but also to sustain circular community engagement locally and provide service support at the city scale destined to policymakers, makerspaces, civil society, industrials. As an example, it can be mentioned the Pop Machina Circular Maker Academy,[12] the development of new Fab City Hub open to public, new local collaborations about biomaterial like Remix the School,[13] new training, incubation and acceleration programs elaborated through EU projects (FoodShift, Centrinno, Shemakes) [21, 25, 27].

---

[12] https://fablabbcn.org/projects/pop-machina.

[13] https://fablabbcn.org/projects/remix-the-school.

5 Lessons Learnt and Reflections

This co-creation journey was a rich learning journey for the participants who could have the chance to experience the benefit of research-action, distributing their time between local co-creation management, activity design and reflective moments with the SISCODE consortium.

The co-creation process also conducted the project members to envision and test a set of indicators to monitor circular community projects emphasising the importance of demonstrating the changes of material flows, being transparent about the state of environmental impact analysis, commenting the learning curves and cross-pollination of knowledge between members, showing the effective interactions between stakeholders and expliciting honestly the capacity of the lab infrastructure to respond to the local needs.

The team entered into the intimacy of the co-creation processes and could have faced many complex situations. Some lessons learnt from this particular case could be noted:

- Co-creation is about creating safe and accessible learning spaces to ensure people have trust in themself, rising autonomy, regardless of their profiles or expertise, while connecting them with ideas and realities, proposing innovative forms of dialoguing with uncertain futures.
- Facilitating co-creation in Labs come with many soft skills to acquire and could benefit from various profiles such as the "gurus", technical experts passionate about making, systemic designers acting as interfaces between people, design artefacts and new policies and community managers that have a natural sense of connecting with people embedded in the local territory.
- Co-creation processes are value-centred. The Remix collective all shares the common motivation to create positive changes, rethinking how to better co-create "commons" through knowledge cross-pollination and learning by doing philosophy, and caring, by being curious and caring about others.

Co-creation is about dealing with creativity, uncertainties and tensions. Constant efforts are being done to reframe the action, maintain the cohesion, dialoguing about potential doubts of participants. Pollinating co-creation processes such as the ones initiated through the Siscode project (letting open spaces for expressing common aspirations and concerns has a strong role in better engaging with citizens and overcoming tensions present in territorial dynamics.

References

1. Agència de Residus de Catalunya—Food waste. http://residus.gencat.cat/en/ambits_dactuacio/prevencio/malbaratament_alimentari. Last accessed 2021/03/29
2. Climate Plan BCN—Climate Plan 2018–2030. https://www.barcelona.cat/barcelona-pel-clima/sites/default/files/documents/climate_plan_maig.pdf. Last accessed 2021/03/29

3. Co-Design with biomaterials from food leftovers in Poblenou—Exhibition catalogue. https://issuu.com/iaac/docs/remix_el_barrio_catalogo_en__1__compressed. Last accessed 2021/03/29
4. Decidim.barcelona. https://www.decidim.barcelona/. Last accessed 2021/03/29
5. Diez T (2018) Fab City Whitepaper Locally productive, globally connected self-sufficient cities Available at: https://fab.city/documents/whitepaper.pdf. Last accessed 2020/06/28
6. Distributed Design Market Platform, https://distributeddesign.eu/. Last accessed 2021/03/29
7. Distributed fab City Summit 2020. https://fablabbcn.org/calendar/fabcitysummit2020. Last accessed 2021/03/29
8. European Commission: A sustainable Bioeconomy for Europe: strengthening the connection between economy, society and the environment. Brussels (2018) https://ec.europa.eu/research/bioeconomy/pdf/ec_bioeconomy_strategy_2018.pdf. Last accessed 2020/06/26
9. Fabricademy. https://textile-academy.org/. Last accessed 2021/06/23
10. Fabtextiles. http://fabtextiles.org/. Last accessed 2021/06/23
11. FoodTech 3.0 Lab—Food Shift. https://foodshift2030.eu/labs/food-tech-3-0-lab/. Last accessed 2021/03/29
12. Foodture Barcelona. http://www.foodture.barcelona/. Last accessed 2021/03/29
13. Gustavsson J, Cederberg C, Sonesson U, Van Otterdijk R, Meybeck A (2011) Global food losses and food waste. Global food losses and food waste—extent, causes and prevention. Rome, available at https://www.madr.ro/docs/ind-alimentara/risipa_alimentara/presentation_food_waste.pdf. Last accessed 2020/08/25
14. Iscape, p—Improving the Smart Control of Air Pollution in Europe, https://www.iscapeproject.eu/. Last accessed 2021/03/29
15. Les cooperatives obreres de Sants [Libro], https://www.freepress.coop/les-cooperatives-obreres-de-sants-libro/. Last accessed 2021/03/29
16. Making Sense EU, http://making-sense.eu/. Last accessed 2021/03/29
17. Materfad. https://www.fad.cat/materfad/es. Last accessed 2021/06/23
18. OECD (2020) The circular economy in cities and regions: synthesis report. OECD Urban Studies. OECD Publishing, Paris
19. Pistofidou A, Real M, Juarez Calvo M (2020) Remix El Barrio: a co-creation journey to foster innovative ecosystems crafting and micro-fabricating with food surplus and waste. Creative Food Cycles-Book 1:185–195
20. Poblenou Urban District. https://www.poblenouurbandistrict.com/es/category/poblenou-urban-district/podn12h/. Last accessed 2021/03/29
21. Pop-Machina – FabLab BCN. https://fablabbcn.org/projects/pop-machina. Last accessed 2021/03/29
22. Real M, Calvo M (2019) Boosting co-creation practices in makespaces to support the design of more empowering and circular food systems at a neighbourhood scale. In: Proceedings of the 19th European roundtable for sustainable consumption and production circular, vol 1, Spain. ISBN 978-84-09-16892-7, pp 831–840
23. Remix el Barrio—Biomaterials Recipe Videos. https://www.youtube.com/playlist?list=PL33KKs9g8Y1K4MJGAUHpMZn-wMcbOVhnV. Last accessed 2021/03/29
24. Remix el Barrio—Gitbook. https://flbcn.gitbook.io/remix-el-barrio/. Last accessed 2021/03/29
25. Remix the school—FabLab BCN. https://fablabbcn.org/projects/remix-the-school. Last accessed 2021/03/29
26. Restaurant Leka, Barcelona. https://restauranteleka.com/. Last accessed 2021/03/29.
27. SheMakes—FabLab BCN. https://fablabbcn.org/projects/shemakes. Last accessed 2021/03/29
28. Starts Prize. https://starts-prize.aec.at/en/. Last accessed 2021/06/23
29. Woods M, Balestrini M, Bejtullahu S, Bocconi S, Boerwinkel G, Boonstra M, Boschman D-S, Camprodon G, Coulson S, Diez T, Fazey I, Hemment D, van den Horn C, Ilazi T, Jansen-Dings I, Kresin F, McQuillan D, Nascimento S, Pareschi E, Polvora A, Salaj R, Scott M, Seiz G, Fazey I (2018) Citizen sensing: a toolkit

Polifactory. Transforming Playful Movement into Sound: Co-create a Smart System for Children with Cerebral Palsy

Carla Sedini, Laura Cipriani, Mirko Gelsomini, Stefano Maffei, and Massimo Bianchini

This chapter explores the potential of co-creation and user innovation, investigating the physical-motor needs of children diagnosed with cerebral palsy with specific attention to the translation of movement in sound stimuli. It describes the co-design and development of BODYSOUND, a smart system that exploits a playful activity to encourage movements and transform them into sound.

1 Introduction

Polifactory (polifactory.polimi.it) is the makerspace and Fab Lab of Politecnico di Milano, created and coordinated by the Department of Design in collaboration with the Departments of Mechanical Engineering and Electronics, Information and Bioengineering. It is an interdisciplinary research lab and an Advanced Technology Centre that explores the relationship between design and new production models working in the fields of digital transformation, circular economy, open and user innovation.

C. Sedini (✉) · L. Cipriani · M. Gelsomini · S. Maffei · M. Bianchini
Department of Design, Politecnico di Milano, Milan, Italy
e-mail: carla.sedini@polimi.it

L. Cipriani
e-mail: laura1.cipriani@polimi.it

M. Gelsomini
e-mail: mirko.gelsomini@polimi.it

S. Maffei
e-mail: stefano.maffei@polimi.it

M. Bianchini
e-mail: massimo.bianchini@polimi.it

© The Author(s) 2022

A. Deserti et al. (eds.), *Co-creation for Responsible Research and Innovation,*
Springer Series in Design and Innovation 15,
https://doi.org/10.1007/978-3-030-78733-2_5

Polifactory develops competitive and experimental research, consultancy projects for large companies and SMEs, experimental didactics, preincubation of talents and ideas for master degree students, PhD candidates, and fellow researchers.

Since 2017 *Polifactory* has begun to develop research processes aimed at studying the ecosystems of bottom-up and participatory innovation in the healthcare sector, such as MakeToCare research [3, 4], in collaboration with Sanofi Genzyme and Fondazione Politecnico, a systemic study of the actors and projects related to patient innovation in Italy.

To develop the SISCODE pilot project, the *Polifactory* team decided to consider the healthcare sector, with specific attention to the physical-motor needs of children diagnosed with cerebral palsy. *Polifactory* addressed its challenge with a service design approach. The final solution, called BODYSOUND, was co-created in collaboration with a wide range of stakeholders: patients (children), caregivers (parents), therapists, policymakers.

The journey was composed of three main phases, during which co-creation activities were carried out. After preliminary research and activities planning, the three main phases officially started in May 2019 and ended in November 2020.

The final solution is BODYSOUND, a system that proposes a new way of performing physical reactivation. It is based on choreutics (a combination of dance and music) and the transformation of movement into sound.

2 Ecosystem, Context and Challenge Addressed

Nowadays, healthcare systems worldwide have been incredibly stressed because of the pandemic. Several weaknesses have emerged and highlighted, in particular, the capacity to respond to emergencies as such in a systemic way, maintaining the provision of cures and support for other' typologies of illness and diseases. When *Polifactory* started its pilot project, which is the topic of this chapter, the pandemic was not diffused yet; however, the challenge and idea appeared lately to fit in this current situation.

Since 1997, Italy has opted for decentralising the healthcare system, giving regions more autonomy shifting towards a "public–private" model (privatisation boomed between 2010 and 2020). In 2014, Lombardy Region published the White Paper on developing the social and health system in Lombardy, followed by the law of reorganisation "Evolution of the Lombardy socio-economic system" (August 2015). In addition to that, Lombardy Region founded the Life Sciences Lombard Cluster, which collects all the public and private actors committed to diagnostics, advanced therapies, pharmaceuticals, medical devices, and technologies applied to health. The Cluster facilitates the progress of life sciences in Lombardy and creates new business opportunities among the members.

At the local level, the Municipality of Milan focuses on lines of action that are influent for *Polifactory* pilot project, such as urban manufacturing, start-ups, and knowledge-intensive economy with particular attention to technological and economic development, social cohesion, and participation in the city.

Although Italy ranked as the world's healthiest country and fourth in the health system efficiency rank [5], there has been a decreasing good health perception. The same happened for the trust in the medical system manifested by the Italian population.

In previous research activities, *Polifactory* carried out several interviews with doctors that confirm data on self-diagnosis; indeed, in many cases, patients, when they do not make the diagnosis and the cure by themselves, tend to adjust and correct the treatment without consulting the doctor first [2]. The habit of independently facing own small health problems is not necessarily bad. Experts speak of a process of "autonomy", which is well evaluated by operators in health policy because it reduces public spending and allows doctors to focus on the most serious pathologies. However, self-managed medicine is neither easy nor risk-free. Makerspaces and Fab Labs can operate as mediators and facilitators in processes of *Patient Innovation* [1, 6, 11]. In order to frame the concept of Patient Innovation it can be referred to the wider concept of Grassroots Innovation, defined as "a network of activists and organisations generating novel bottom-up solutions for sustainable development and sustainable consumption; solutions that respond to the local situation and the interests and values of the communities involved" [8]. The common characteristics which define a "low level" of Patient Innovation solutions can be summed up as follows. They are independent and personal because often developed to face individual issues; they are "redundant" because often the solution identified already existed; they are shared since often patients tend to share their positive experience with other people in their same condition. Makerspaces and Fab Labs can operate as mediators and facilitators in these processes to reach higher levels of Patient Innovation. Within this panorama, Italian and especially Milanese makerspaces and creative communities are particularly active in projects that deal with healthcare. Italian fablabs collaborate and operate on these issues together with patient associations, policymakers and RRI experts in several European projects, such as FabCare and MakeToCare (*Polifactory*); Made4You, Hackability Milano (OpenDot); OpenCare (WeMake); Ubora (Fab Lab Pisa), etc.

Looking at future policies, they would "enable or encourage more innovation effort investment by users at either the extensive (i.e. having more users engage in innovation or innovation diffusion) or intensive (i.e. enabling users that already innovate or diffuse innovations to invest greater efforts in doing so)" [9].

For these reasons, the challenge has been framed in the domain of healthcare and wellbeing. In particular, it was decided to focus on infantile Cerebral Palsy (CP), one of the most common physical disabilities in childhood: 2–2.5 per 1000 new borns and children are affected by CP (esteem of 3 per 1000 in Milan). Notwithstanding the diffusion of infantile CP, there is a lack of knowledge on it, and it is threatened as a rare disease: the public welfare system poorly sustains it, and informal caregivers (parents) are not supported or trained in managing their children' problems.

FightTheStroke was identified as the patients and caregivers association with whom to collaborate. It deals and operates with and for young stroke survivors with a disability of infantile CP and their families; it was crucial to know the issue better and contact families and therapists. Thanks to the dialogue with the president of the association and a survey carried out with parents of children affected with CP, the final challenge of *Polifactory* was identified: addressing the physical-motor needs of children diagnosed with CP, exploring them according to proprioception principles with specific attention to translating movement into sound stimuli.

3 The Co-creation Journey

Polifactory's co-creation journey was composed of the following stages, which were conducted recursively:

- analysis: survey and interviews
- ideation: co-design and experimentation workshops
- prototyping: three loops of development and tests.

Stakeholders involved are listed in Table 1, according to their participation in the different phases.

Thanks to the survey and the initial encounter with FightTheStroke, *Polifactory* reframed its challenge. It was decided to work on sports and play, focusing in particular on music because, as Rosenbaum and Gorter state [7], based on The International Classification of Functioning, Disability and Health (ICF) from the World Health Organisation, a true and effective global takeover of the child must give importance to a series of factors, described through six simple words, the so-called 6 F-Words: function, family, fitness, fun, friends, future [10].

Three co-design and experimental workshops were conducted during the ideation phase to validate some intuitions, refine the needs, and better identify the various stakeholder groups' effective problems. Thanks to the first cycle of workshops, needs and—subsequential—design opportunities were identified. *Polifactory* researchers refined and systematised the ideas that emerged during debrief moments, originating one singular idea: BODYSOUND.

The second cycle of workshops tried to verify it. The solution was presented to the participants, who imagined a user journey for it. In particular, they appreciated the systematisation of several ideas together, and they were able to discuss barriers and

Table 1 Project phases and stakeholder engagement

	Patients	Caregivers	Therapists	Policymakers
Analysis		X	X	X
Ideation 1st cycle	X			X
Ideation 2nd cycle	X			X
Ideation 3rd cycle	X			X
Ideation 4th cycle	X			X

opportunities of the solution. From this second cycle emerged the concept of a virtual system where gamification elements help the motor stimulation and—possibly—reactivate the limbs. The result may occur by encouraging the children/users to use and move the plegic part by executing a series of choreographies.

The third cycle of workshops was organised after the first prototyping loop of the solution. Indeed, BODYSOUND prototyping followed a *quick and dirt* development approach, which is very useful for anticipating results and reviewing them during the early stages of work. Several versions ready to be tested were released, even if incompleted. The solution was refined according to tests feedback and co-design results. The last co-design workshop, which *Polifactory* conducted, was aimed at the design of BODYSOUND service. Both caregivers, therapists, and policymakers participated in this last workshop. The participants had to hypothesise the provider of the service, specific software functions and goals. Two primary "environments" (providers) were identified: schools and sports centers; however, the main idea did not change very much according to the various locations. As for the first co-design workshop, the debrief phase was crucial for identifying strengths and weaknesses and merging the most promising features into one unique idea.

The COVID-19 pandemic influenced BODYSOUND journey, and the core team had to review it according to the impossibility of being in the same place at the same time. In particular, *Polifactory* conducted the prototyping activities remotely, but to maintain the users' involvement, the team had to change the supporting technologies. It was decided to substitute the Kinect with an ordinary webcam to share BODYSOUND with the children who could test it (and use it) from their homes. Before starting this new testing phase, therapists, who participated in the journey, were invited to register the training gestures on a platform ad hoc developed. *Polifactory* did not abandon the original idea but decided to develop *BODYSOUND web* first, a more pervasive and accessible solution at the expense of accuracy, and then *BODYSOUND pro*.

4 Experimentation: Output, Transformations, Outcomes

BODYSOUND System proposes a new way of performing physical reactivation. It is based on choreutics (dance and music) through the transformation of movement into sound.

Within this system, children can perform a choreography and transform it into a melody. The system can detect the child's movement and collect information on his/her performances and improvements. Two types of solutions have been designed: *BODYSOUND web* and *BODYSOUND pro*.

First solution—BODYSOUND web
This solution (Fig. 1) is addressed to both patients and caregivers. It is developed for home training and can be used on any device with an internet connection equipped with a webcam (PC or tablet). It does not require installation but only the registration

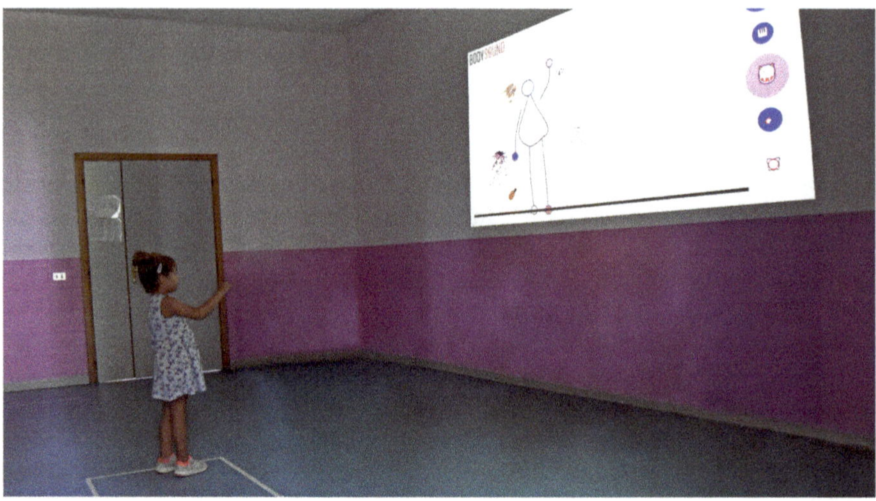

Fig. 1 Bodysound web, testing phase

of a user profile. This version is released with a finite number of exercises, which may vary due to the software updates.

Second solution—BODYSOUND pro
The solution (Fig. 2) is addressed to specialists in the medical, health, and sports field. It is tailored for training sessions to be carried out at schools or sport centers. The system integrates everything necessary (computer, Kinect, projector,…) to set up a space dedicated to the activity to make it accessible to more users simultaneously. This configuration allows the user to load custom movement sequences converted into exercise / game models.

Thanks to SISCODE experience, *Polifactory* improved its capacity to work in multidisciplinary teams and with an interdisciplinary approach since IT and sociology became part of the process. In addition to this, *Polifactory* acquired extended capacities to communicate and collaborate with various stakeholders. Furthermore, special attention has been dedicated to children as the main target. *Polifactory* had never worked with children before. It was a significant experience and opportunity for the team members to acquire competencies in engaging with specific groups of stakeholders.

Co-creation has already been closely linked to Politecnico's culture; however, thanks to SISCODE, Polifatory improved its application and deepened its knowledge of co-creation practices.

The introduction of this new knowledge also enlarged the stakeholder network of *Polifactory*, establishing new relationships and improving the existing ones with policymakers and patients associations. It opened up new possibilities and pathways towards the ideation and development of new experimentation research projects.

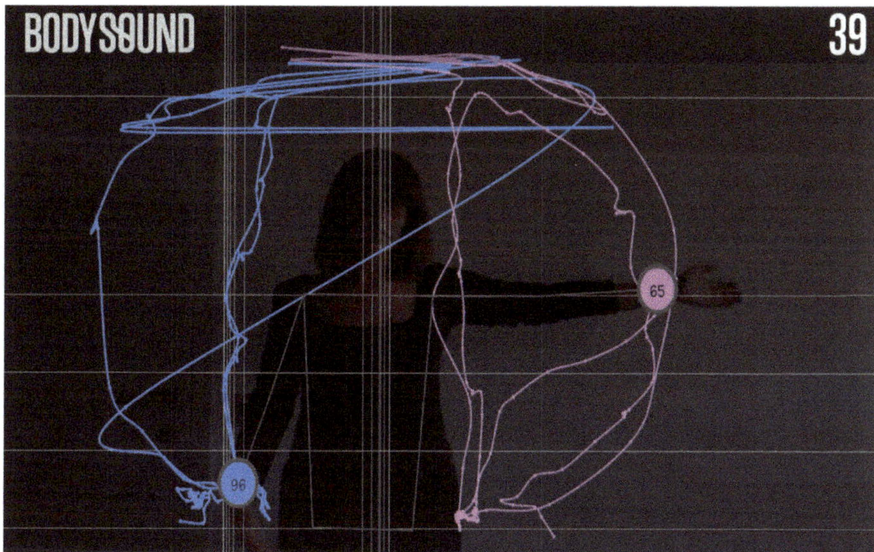

Fig. 2 Bodysound pro, testing phase

It is essential to look at small changes in the whole ecosystem, especially on the accumulative improvements that a pilot project such as BODYSOUND can have. In particular, stressing the relevance of co-creation in healthcare and wellbeing and the unique and crucial role that makerspace and Fab Labs can play in facilitating these processes. Some of the policymakers involved had never participated in activities like these before, providing several positive feedback. At the same time, the capacity of creating a "safe room" for users with specific needs, particularly vulnerable groups, to encounter other stakeholders like policymakers in leading positions was for sure a very relevant and trigger point. The COVID-19 situation stressed the importance of taking care of people with disabilities or in particular health conditions by distance, especially when it is impossible to attend rehabilitation and sports activities.

5 Lessons Learnt and Reflections

Thanks to the pilot project experience, *Polifactory* understood and verified that co-creation processes are highly dependent on the issues faced and their context. Co-designing with vulnerable users needs a different approach than more conventional users' co-creation processes.

The team decided to initially meet the stakeholders in dedicated and private moments because of the delicate and intimate issue and to organise lately a collective moment with all the stakeholders involved to build trust among all the participants. As researchers, the team identified the importance of the role of the mediator between different groups. However, additional mediators are crucial in facilitating the relationship between the research group and the main users. In the pilot project, the patient association had a relevant role in contacting and involving parents and children. Concerning building trust, it is essential to share knowledge from both sides, which means that—avoiding biases—researchers have to inform participants and keep them informed throughout the whole co-creation journey regardless of their rank or role outside of the project. Unfortunately, the COVID emergency diminished the possibility of having face-to-face moments of interaction identified as very relevant. Apart from participating in operative workshops, informal conversations were necessary to share opinions, build trust, and observe how interaction dynamics are performed. Therefore, the space of interaction is very relevant as well. Also, relaxing moments (such as lunches or coffee breaks) need to be organised and managed to facilitate exchanges and keep up the "safe space" created during the activities. Talking about the co-creation workshops is possible to say that they were all organised according to three main activities:

1. share information, knowledge, and experiences
2. hands and minds on: imagine possible scenarios and solutions through the use of co-design tools
3. reflect (and share again): collectively analyse the solution identified and select the best ones.

Finally, respect is one of the most relevant factors to consider: stakeholders have their commitments, and time is one of the most precious resources. Thus, it is crucial to give value to the time they donate.

To sum up, *Polifactory* identified four main elements characterising a co-creation journey:

- it is an accumulative and iterative process
- it needs to pay attention to time and space issues
- it requires the researcher to be a mediator
- it has to keep stakeholders informed throughout the whole process.

References

1. DeMonaco H, Oliveira P, Torrance A, von Hippel C, von Hippel E (2019) When patients become innovators. MIT Sloan Manag Rev. https://sloanreview.mit.edu/article/when-patients-become-innovators/. Last accessed 2021/03/28
2. Eurispes: Rapporto Italia 2017 (2017)
3. Maffei S, Bianchini M, Parini B, Delli Zotti E (2017) MakeToCare. An ecosystem of actors and user-centered innovation for the innovation in the field of healthcare. Libraccio Editore, Milano
4. Maffei S, Bianchini M, Parini B, Cipriani L (2019) MakeToCare2. La patient innovation in Italia tra progetto e mercato. Libraccio Editore, Milano

5. Miller LJ, Lu W (2018) These are the economies with the most (and least) efficient health care. Available at https://www.bloomberg.com/news/articles/2018-09-19/u-s-near-bottom-of-health-index-hong-kong-and-singapore-at-top. Last accessed 2021/03/28
6. Oliveira P, Zejnilovic L, Canhão H, von Hippel E (2014) Patient innovation under rare diseases and chronic needs. Orphanet J Rare Dis 9(1):850
7. Rosenbaum P, Gorter JW (2012) The 'F-words' in childhood disability: I swear this is how we should think! Child: Care, Health Dev 38(4):457–463
8. Seyfang G, Smith A (2007) Grassroots innovations for sustainable development: towards a new research and policy agenda. Environ Polit 16(4):584–603
9. Svensson PO, Hartmann RK (2018) Policies to promote user innovation: Makerspaces and clinician innovation in Swedish hospitals. Res Policy 47(1):277–288
10. WHO (2001) World Health Organisation international classification of functioning. Disability and Health, Geneva
11. Zejnilovic L, Oliveira P, Canhão H (2016) Innovations by and for patients, and their place in the future health care system. In: Pinkwart A, Meffert H, Albach H, Reichwald R, von Eiff E (eds) Boundaryless hospital: rethink and redefine health care management. Springer, Berlin

Maker—Plastic In, Plastic Out: Circular Economy and Local Production

Asger Nørregård-Rasmussen, Malte Hertz-Jansen, and Felicitas Schmittinger

Recognising the lack of local and economically accessible facilities, technologies, and public engagement in local recycling, the chapter tackles the challenge of introducing Circular Economy to cope with plastic waste in Copenhagen. The need for circular systemic innovation and holistic production models for recycling plastics led to consider how local micro entrepreneurs, SMEs, commercial resellers and citizens can collaborate for a common, sustainable goal. The chapter presents 'Plastic In, Plastic Out' (PIPO), a Circular system for local sourcing, recycling and production of sustainable plastic building materials and products.

1 Introduction

The organisation

Maker is a FabLab located in Copenhagen (Denmark) with a focus on local production, circular economy and the democratisation of knowledge.

Founded in 2015 it addressed challenges of local and national relevance by fostering the maker-ecosystem and creating and nourishing a network among makers, enterprises, public entities, civil society and policymakers.

This is established by applying the co-creation approach to the development of new, sustainable solutions applying design thinking tools and building new capacities

A. Nørregård-Rasmussen (✉) · M. Hertz-Jansen
Maker/Viadukten, Copenhagen, Denmark
e-mail: asger@maker-effekt.dk

M. Hertz-Jansen
e-mail: malte@maker-effekt.dk

F. Schmittinger
Department of Design, Politecnico di Milano, Milan, Italy
e-mail: felicitas.schmittinger@polimi.it

A. Deserti et al. (eds.), *Co-creation for Responsible Research and Innovation*,
Springer Series in Design and Innovation 15,
https://doi.org/10.1007/978-3-030-78733-2_6

in relation to the co-creation of solutions, prototyping and the application of new technologies.

Maker supports makers and entrepreneurs as well as local actors and stakeholders in Denmark as a mediator fostering formal and informal connections and relationships contributing to strengthen local landscapes of stakeholders in Denmark.

The co-creation journey

The provisioning, consumption and disposal of rising amounts of resources is immensely challenging countries and regions worldwide. Denmark, and Copenhagen in particular, counts a waste production per capita double the European average [1] leading to the development of the Resource and Waste Management Plan 24 (RAP 24) that clearly states the pressing need for change in the following years [2, 3].

At the same time, alternative models for the local production and recycling of resources are emerging and citizen-driven initiatives have started tackling the issue.

Maker addresses this need for more sustainable solutions with a focus on circular economy instead of traditional linear production chains. Aiming to enhance local cooperation and collaboration and the involvement of fablab and maker communities, the prototype takes a focus on the creation of a new approach towards a community-driven ecosystem enabling new models and systems for the recycling of plastic waste.

It was developed over the course of 21 months by analysing the current local systems and infrastructures to create a shared knowledge base and elaborate a new, integrated ecosystem of stakeholders in Copenhagen.

'Plastic In, Plastic Out' (PIPO) integrates with the existing ecosystem offering an alternative value-chain by producing plastic sheets and products made of recycled plastic combining the reuse, recycling, manufacturing and consumption by adopting a local and systemic approach.

2   Ecosystem, Context and Challenge Addressed

Ecosystem

Denmark's recycling rate is lower than the average in Europe, especially the direct recycling and re-use of materials is complicated by a variety of legislative obstacles omitting the development of local recycling systems.

It has been acknowledged that not only legislative change is needed, but also the socio-cultural aspect and the specificities of the local contexts and environments need to be taken into account when moving towards the more efficient use of resources.

These particular contexts need to be explored and understood in depth to then develop new technical and innovative solutions to foster the ongoing trend of recycling the highest amount of waste possible through the improvement of waste sorting and management that has risen from 27 to over 45% in the last years in the city of Copenhagen showing a positive trend [2].

The concrete goals of the city to improve the use of resources and waste throughout the next year aligns *Maker's* goals with the local agendas producing a series of other activities and projects with similar scopes to jointly obtain an adaptation of limiting regulations related to regulations for material reuse, certifications and material transparency.

The political landscape is currently undergoing an important process of transformation acknowledging not only the importance to adapt policies, but also to involve citizens and stakeholders to provoke behavioural change and collaboration among the actors towards a common goal.

Organisational context

Maker as a FabLab has varied experiences in facilitating and fostering cross-sector collaboration to promote entrepreneurship, open source management and initiatives related to circular economy.

As a part of the maker movement and the FabLab network since 2015, the 'maker mindset' consists of elements from design thinking, prototyping and iterative design methods applied regularly both for the exploration of topics and the validation of concepts.

A wide variety of stakeholders are involved in their projects ranging from architects and designers to civil servants and policymakers. The aforementioned 'maker mindset' and their set of collaborative techniques and tools allow the collaboration in a wide network of different stakeholders exploiting and integrating varied knowledge and experiences to develop solutions collaboratively.

Co-creation and co-design as well as a variety of prototyping techniques are applied in formal or informal, iterative processes that are adapted to the specific project and stakeholders involved to create common ground.

Challenge

Starting from the Fab City agenda, *Maker* aimed to develop a small-scale circular ecosystem with a high potential for replication and scaling establishing a community for local production and circular economy [4]. Having identified the increasing requests for locally produced plastic together with a rising number of designers and makers buying recycled plastic sheets from the UK-based company SMILE plastics.

Maker's challenge consists in developing new possibilities for local recycling of plastic waste in Copenhagen by addressing the lack of adequate facilities, knowhow and entire systems of recycling and production of new materials.

An entirely new chain of production needs to be developed identifying generators of plastic waste to opportunities for recycling and the creation of new materials for the use and processing of these materials taking an entirely new chain and ecosystem of recycling and production into account.

3 The Co-creation Journey

3.1 Context Analysis

Starting from a desk research on the various aspects of the chosen issue like circular economy, plastic production, recycling of plastic, community-driven solutions, development plans and strategies and the national and regional legislations in relation to them, already a number of stakeholders from industry and the innovation community have been involved.

The identified stakeholders and stakeholder groups have then been mapped within an ecosystem model dividing them into categories (Fig. 1) and to be updated after every step of the co-creation process.

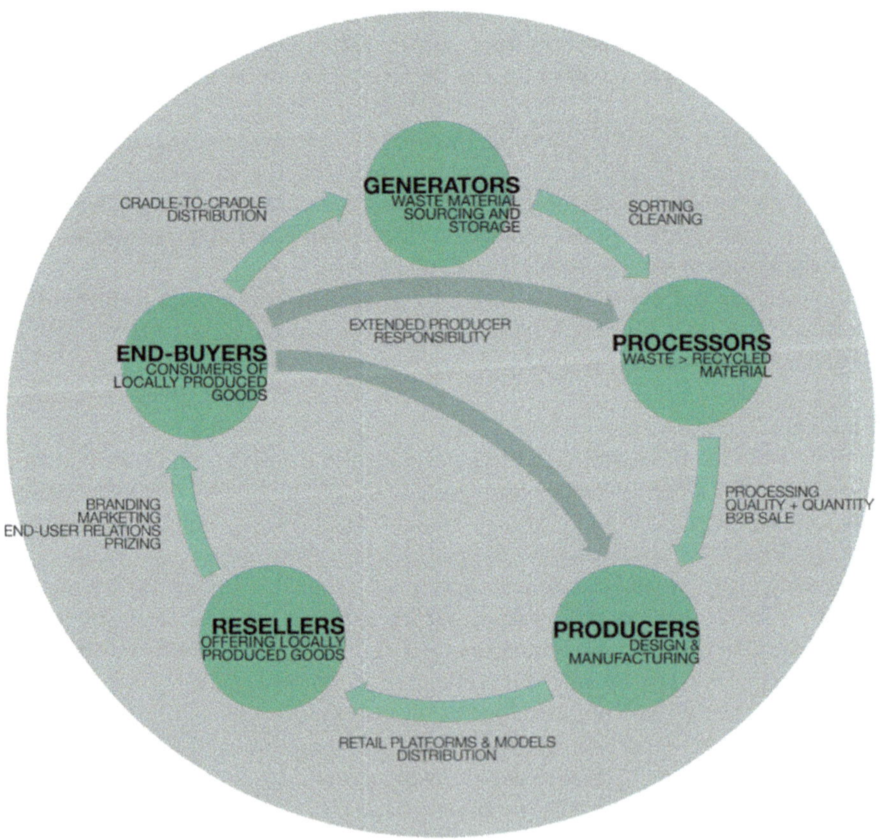

Fig. 1 Initial draft of a local cradle-to-cradle ecosystem model (Elaborated by Stine Broen Christensen)

Further field research conducted through interviews, workshops and field visits led to further definition of the context and field of research to frame the precise challenge and build a common base to start developing a common solution.

Problem reframing

The problem has been precisely defined according to three main points:

1. Theoretical aspects and agenda from the Fab City initiative—i.e. creating more livable cities and community focused descriptions [4].
2. Direct feedback on the effective scaling opportunities, industry collaborations and technical solutions.
3. A shared intent to focus more on empowerment, community building, open access to knowledge and learnings.

In collaboration with a group of students, the entire lifecycle of plastic has been investigated and assessed to then interact with industrial stakeholders and public employees to grasp the challenge from a variety of different perspectives conducting a series of workshops, interviews and informal meetings (Fig. 2).

Envisioning of alternatives

Starting from a series of prototyping activities for the recycling and reuse of plastic the phase of solution development has been initiated.

Fig. 2 Game and stakeholder mapping by AAU students & Maker

A set of co-design workshops, a maker meet-up and an open lab day have been organised to refine the concept and make concrete plans for the prototyping phase as well as aligning the solution to the needs of all stakeholders.

In this phase, also the FabCity initiative has been involved again through talks at the Open Lab Day to reconnect the prototype to their general agenda and inspire local stakeholders.

In this process, the concept has been narrowed down with a focus on the recycling of plastic for the co-production of recycled plastic sheets and their processing into products integrating this new ecosystem in the current network of circular economy in Copenhagen aligning it with existing initiatives, municipal projects and creating collaborative relations with the involved stakeholders (Fig. 3).

Development and prototyping

The prototyping process underwent several iterations to improve both the plastic sheets as the produced material and core of the prototype as well as the ecosystem developed to meet all stakeholders' needs.

9 different products have been produced locally from the plastic sheets that then have been showcased in an exhibition taking place digitally due to the COVID-19 pandemic.

Apart from the incubation of the production of new objects made from recycled plastic, *Maker* closely collaborated with the industry and innovation community as well as policymakers organising educational activities and co-design workshops engaging more than 150 participants. This has supported the integration with

Fig. 3 Maker Meet Up and Open Lab Day in May 2019

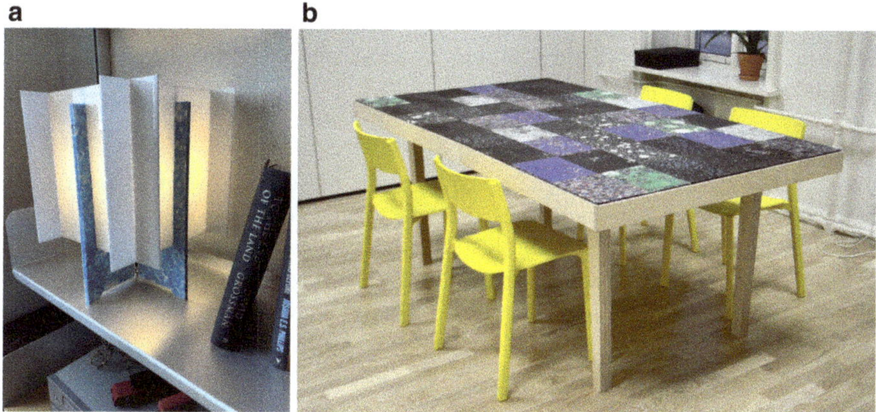

Fig. 4 **a**, **b** Projects developed as part of the prototype

local agendas and initiatives while raising awareness on the need for policy change, building a community and identifying challenges and opportunities for scaling and replication (Fig. 4).

4 Experimentation: Output, Transformations, Outcomes

PIPO stands for 'Plastic In, Plastic Out' and describes a new ecosystem model for small-scale circular economy for the recycling and reuse of plastic with local actors. It aims to connect local initiatives to municipal agendas while showcasing concrete results in a gallery of prototypes to inspire and further develop the use of the material. It functions as an example as a part of the FabCity initiative as well as a way of introducing circular economy in a specific context in an ecosystem empowering local makers and designers.

Transformations

Maker as an organisation has faced a large impact on a strategic level leading to a reorientation towards circular economy and community building through co-creation caused by the project. The previous experience with cross-sector collaborations and co-creation has been enriched and strengthened by the provided framework and training leading to an internal professionalisation and establishment of practices.

Furthermore, the organisation has established new networks and contacts fostering a multi-stakeholder environment and creating a perspective for future collaborations and projects.

The project led to a raised awareness of plastic waste and opportunities to tackle the issue within the core group of stakeholders triggering a series of similar initiatives and considerations for replication.

The COVID-19 pandemic has significantly challenged the execution and activities enabling flexibility, alternative solutions and capacity to cope with challenges and complexity.

Scaling

Being based on the overall challenge to fight plastic waste on a large scale, considerations have been made on scaling the locally developed systems.

The main aim is to exploit the learnings and knowledge gained for the development of other circular models, reuse the process developed in other projects and provide this knowledge open access to empower other communities to establish similar ecosystems.

The scaling of the material as the technical part of the solution has been assigned less importance in this case following an analysis of potential and possibilities with stakeholders and policymakers identifying the difficulty of scaling 'maker solutions' to an industrial level and recognising the development of the ecosystem as the more promising part of the developed solution.

5 Lessons Learnt and Reflections

Co-creation has been identified as a trigger not only to guide activities, but to generate interest by fostering communication, cooperation and inspiration. For the co-creation activities conducted, the importance and benefits of the variety of tools provided has resulted as fundamental in supporting the planning, leading and guidance of workshops and sessions.

Tensions and difficulties of communication among stakeholders and stakeholder groups have been traced back to their inequality in terms of levels and positions raising the need to implement further mechanisms to balance this contrast.

The difficulties in engaging policymakers as a stakeholder group resulted as a barrier, since their engagement at the same time has been found crucial to shape a realistic and implementable solution.

References

1. Danmark Uden Affald: genanvend mere - forbrænd mindre. Miljøstyrelsen MST 2011, https://mst.dk/media/mst/Attachments/MST_Faktaark_1_WEB.pdf. Last accessed 2021/01/05
2. Cirkulær København: Resource- og Affaldsplan 2024. Københavns Kommune 2019, https://kk.sites.itera.dk/apps/kk_pub2/index.asp?mode=detalje&id=1990. Last accessed 2021/01/05
3. KBH 2025 Klimaplanen - Københavns Kommune 2012, https://kk.sites.itera.dk/apps/kk_pub2/index.asp?mode=detalje&id=1035. Last accessed 2021/01/05
4. Diez et al. Fab City Whitepaper: Locally productive, globally connected self-sufficient cities, https://fab.city/uploads/whitepaper.pdf. Last accessed 2021/01/05

KTP—Collectively Improving Air Quality in Krakow: A New Air Quality Plan for the Małopolska Region

Agnieszka Włodarczyk-Gębik, Aleksandra Gabriel, Maria Dubis, and Monika Machowska

KTP's project relates to the challenge of air pollution and the need to improve quality of life in Kraków and the Kraków Metropolitan Area. The aim is to improve the quality of the air by motivating citizens to change their ecological attitudes, transport and heating habits and support decision makers with relevant tools and instruments for better co-creation of local new policies with a user-centered approach. The chapter describes the preparation of the new Air Quality Plan for Małopolska, and the creation of a common space for citizens, policymakers, entrepreneurs and other stakeholders where self-development, realisation and business take place.

1 Introduction

The Kraków Technology Park (*KTP*) is a leading technology park in Poland. It is the most complete business one-stop-shop operating in the Małopolska Region, in the south of Poland. With entrepreneurs, academia, and territorial authorities, the *KTP* created a unique and dynamic ecosystem to boost the regional economy. The core area of its operations are IT and ICT, and e-driven solutions. As a business innovation centre, *KTP* directly supports over 150 innovative hi-tech startups and SMEs and 170

A. Włodarczyk-Gębik (✉) · A. Gabriel · M. Dubis · M. Machowska
Krakowski Park Technologiczny, Krakow, Poland
e-mail: awlodarczyk@kpt.krakow.pl

A. Gabriel
e-mail: agabriel@kpt.krakow.pl

M. Dubis
e-mail: mdubis@kpt.krakow.pl

M. Machowska
e-mail: mmachowska@kpt.krakow.pl

© The Author(s) 2022

A. Deserti et al. (eds.), *Co-creation for Responsible Research and Innovation,*
Springer Series in Design and Innovation 15,
https://doi.org/10.1007/978-3-030-78733-2_7

other manufacturing companies from different sectors (i.e. software, Industry 4.0, automotive, cybersecurity, aerospace, engineering, BPO/SSC, FMCG) in the special economic zone and Polish Investment Zone. Around 40 startups and 40 mature companies, mainly SMEs (active in Industry 4.0, IoT, automotive, software, games, cybersecurity, Smart City, spacetech and other industries) work in the park's office spaces. The *KTP* cooperates with over 100 partners on international and national projects financed from such programmes as Interreg, Horizon 2020, Erasmus+, and national and regional ones.

The *KTP* is well recognised on both regional and international levels for being a key actor in co-creating and implementing the Regional Innovation Strategy and promoting smart specialisation and user-driven innovation approaches in the region. Two of the many initiatives run by the *KTP* are certainly worth mentioning: the Kraków Living Lab (est. 2015) and the Digital Innovation Hub (est. 2019). The KTP is also an active member of EBN, IASP, ENoLL, and SOOIIP networks.

The company has been involved in an array of activities and projects dealing with climate change and air pollution issues, among others SMART KOM and SISCODE projects. These are umbrella projects for actions aimed at raising awareness of climate change issues among decision makers and supporting start-ups and SMEs that deliver smart products and services to fight climate change.

The KTP introduced innovative methods, including webinars and such digital tools as mural, miro and deskle, to strengthen and enrich cooperation with stakeholders [2]. It also organises hackathons, workshops and other events presenting best practices in public innovation. The KTP is also experienced in developing e-learning platforms.

2 Ecosystem, Context and Challenge Addressed

The Polish National Air Pollution Control Programme is a document that regulates issues connected to air pollution in Poland. It lays a special emphasis on areas of high pollutant concentration and high population density, as air pollution in those areas has a major impact on resident health and life. Poland is obliged to observe EU law to meet the goals defined by the World Health Organisation by 2030 [6]. These laws urge Poland—even more intensive work is done for the sake of clean air, which is one of the greatest ecological challenges of these days.

A large share of the responsibility to meet the obligations and improve the quality of air throughout the country is vested in the regions, self-governments, decision-makers, and the residents themselves. It is only through the cooperation between these groups and through a joint effort that the defined goal—improvement of air quality—can be achieved, and the general awareness can be improved. In Poland, each region must create a plan for protecting air quality. If such a plan is to answer the real needs of the population, it has to be discussed and consulted in more extensive circles of representatives of business, administration, the civil society, academia, and the local residents together.

The Małopolska Region has designed a strategic act officially functioning as the Air Quality Plan (also called air protection plan) [1]. It is an act of law in force until 2023 that contains the descriptions of long-term remedial activities, a plan for short-term actions that includes:

- introduction of grading for air pollution dangers
- fine-tuning of questions connected to the stocktaking of emission sources
- quality analysis
- description of economic, environmental, and local conditions and circumstances
- selected courses of remedial actions, and
- introduction of control tools and instruments to allow an efficient implementation of the programme.

Important for the region, this publication contains specific goals both for the long and short terms, e.g. the introduction of warnings issued when pollution reaches certain levels, and recording and stocktaking of emission sources.

The strategy was developed in cooperation with the Kraków Technology Park, which joined the project in January 2019, becoming actively involved in the process of consulting the programme with representatives of non-governmental organisations, experts, scientists, civil servants, representatives of business, and primarily with local residents [3]. For the first time, such extensive and open consultations with the civil society were organised around the creation of regional documents.

It is also the first such programme to provide a tangible support tool for households, namely co-financing of modernisation of heating sources. Moreover, the local communities were offered support from a group of specialised environmental experts. They helped to streamline the process and advise the locals on how to embrace the change in the best way possible and how to adjust their homesteads to it.

The work of the environmental consultants has already brought the first results: the concentration of PM 10 (particulate matter) in the heating season lasting from October 2019 to March 2020 dropped by 30% compared to the same period in 2014/15 [5].

The support of the Kraków Technology Park helped to create a true-to-life, fact-based strategic document reflecting the needs and expectations of broad stakeholder groups that is highly feasible, measurable, and scalable.

The work has brought good effects, however the design team also faced challenges. The first was to create the programme with such an extensive range of stakeholders, often with opposing expectations and demands. The other was to found the document on credible data, with assumptions that could be measurable and scalable. It is worth emphasising that apart from the work on the development of the new Air Quality Program, the KPT team was also involved in the coordination of works on the implementation of a platform for monitoring industrial pollution [4]. It was the winning project of the hackathon dedicated to the solutions for improving air quality that the KPT co-organised in December 2019. Implementation of that solution included tests with final users, that is people living in the municipality, and representatives of the production facilities located on its territory.

3 The Co-creation Journey

The project aimed at the development of an open and transparent environment for the development of the Air Quality Programme for the Małopolska Region. A very important aspect within it was to understand the needs and expectations of the stakeholders, and involve them into the creation of the best solutions for the improvement of quality of life. The journey from concept to the creation of a solution lasted for 18 months, and included intensive work with representatives of local authorities and the consumers of the solution.

To ensure the widest possible insight into the residents' opinions on air quality issues, the Kraków Technology Park planned and conducted a series of four co-creation workshops organised in the Living Lab methodology. They provided an open forum of dialogue for people interested and involved in the improvement of air quality in Małopolska. The goal of the workshop was to analyse together the factors and issues that cause poor air quality in the region, and to work out suggestions for solutions that should be introduced sooner or later to improve the status quo. The workshops turned out project fiches that are a significant contribution to the consultation process for updating the Air Quality Plan.

Additionally, to reinforce the diagnosis and to learn the opinions of the residents of the Kraków Metropolitan Area, the Kraków Technology Park conducted two workshops with residents of two smaller communes from the Kraków Metropolitan Area.

The workshops with participation of representatives of the locals, non-governmental organisations, academia, business, and territorial governments, were held from March to April 2019.

The co-creation workshops with participation of the residents of Małopolska initiated an open process of dialogue and exchange of positions and experiences between representatives of various social and professional groups. Thanks to the application of the design thinking method in the process of co-creating the innovative tools and instruments for combating smog, a creative approach to problem solving and creation of new innovative solutions and projects was implemented. Such an approach allows to consider further even those ideas that are hardly rational and feasible, and yet bear a high potential of creativity. Participants of the process actively created innovative and unorthodox solutions, and, by talking and listening to one another, were able to expand the spectrum of understanding of the context of the problem, gaining a fresh insight into specific circumstances, and also to redefine the problem to propose new solutions. These solutions were subjected neither to expert assessment nor voting, and although the ideas were taken down and presented during the wrap-up session, and accounted for in the detailed report that covers general and specific recommendations for the new programme being developed for the Marshal's Office of the Małopolska Region.

The first workshop was conducted in five parallel groups. The objective was to understand the situation of individual persona representative for the residents of Małopolska. The product of the workshop was the definition of key challenges that the people of Małopolska grapple with in the context of air quality and the areas that require intervention. Workshop participants proposed a great deal of potential solutions, and those considered most innovative and feasible were chosen from among their number.

Moreover, the information delivered by people resident in the Kraków Metropolitan Area was used to create a catalogue of good practices and ideas for the future, to be implemented in both short and long perspective.

Then the KPT team created three thematic categories, to which the ideas obtained were assigned. They are: Mobility and public transport, Efficient communication and information, and Monitoring and control.

The work during the second workshop ran in parallel sessions in three thematic groups corresponding to the scopes listed above. As the result, the participants worked out eight detailed concepts for action in the form of project fiches:

- Category: Mobility and public transport (sustainable public transport and low emissions zone in transport)

    - Project: Clean transport zone
    - Project: Metropolitan transport

- Category: Efficient communication and information (how to inform efficiently about the duties imposed by the resolution, and how to persuade to have them implemented in the shortest possible time)

    - Project: Creation of a model community approach to the problem of smog, case study of Skała municipality
    - Project: Involvement of the Roman Catholic Church in fighting smog
    - Project: "I don't believe in smog" information campaign
    - Project: Educational activity in schools

- Category: Monitoring and control (how to monitor efficiently the implementation of the resolution and control infringements of the law)

    - Project: Standardising the system of control in the Małopolska Region
    - Project: Educational aspect of controls.

One of the main courses of activities furthering air quality improvement listed in the Air Quality Plan for Małopolska Region is the reduction of industrial emissions to the environment, and another—ecological education for the locals. An efficient system for monitoring industrial pollution will make it possible to obtain reliable knowledge in the area, and to react quickly and adequately to environmentally adverse developments. These recommendations were aligned with the suggestions of the participants in the co-creation workshops on the reinforcement of monitoring and control competences and efficiency of action that the KPT conducted.

Answering that need, the Kraków Technology Park became involved in the co-organisation of Smogathon. The winner of the hackathon organised in December 2019 and dedicated to working out innovative solutions supporting the fight against smog, was the solution proposed by Qubit team, who prepared the concept of an online platform for monitoring industrial pollution. The prize for the winning team was the implementation of the project in one of Małopolska municipalities. The pilot implementation of their solution was conducted in the municipality of Skawina, after prior reconnaissance of the interest and potential in other communes in the Kraków Metropolitan area. After eight months of co-creation work and preparation, the platform was launched officially. The pilot project on monitoring industrial pollution was presented on the official website of the Małopolska Region and tests were conducted from August to December 2020. That pilot implementation became a tangible effect of the co-creation journey.

Thanks to the pilot solution conducted in that municipality, data from 50 companies were used to identify key challenges connected to the systemic approach to controlling and monitoring industrial pollution on the regional scale. It was very important to have it tested in real life with the locals and potential users.

Such "in-vivo" tests made it possible to winnow both the technical and content errors on the platform, but also to listen to the expectations of the consumers of such a tool. Often both the feedback and the comments surprised both platform developers and the KPT team working on its final shape. Tester comments made it possible to implement an "out of the box" approach, which is hard to obtain while creating so demanding projects in such a short time. The platform was divided into the resident zone and the industrial zone, which were adjusted to user groups and their reasons to use it.

The platform of Qubit team is the other deliverable of the programme. Its improvement will continue so that it can be introduced in other Polish regions. The young innovator team has already entered the concept into their business plan, and are now eagerly pursuing it.

The process of co-creation ended in success both on the public and administrative, and the private local levels. Moderated and co-managed by the Kraków Technology Park, this process of co-creation is an example of well conducted and implemented public–private partnership, in which either party obtains measurable benefits, being at the same time open and ready to give up infeasible claims. Added value that serves the whole region has been created thanks to the mutual understanding of the needs, different standpoints, expectations, and also barriers of legal, cultural and technological nature. The newly designed Air Quality Plan, accounting for the majority of the comments and suggestions submitted during the consultation phase, has been approved, and a prototype of a practical tool for reporting and monitoring ecological incidents has been delivered for the use of the locals and production facilities.

4　Experimentation: Output, Transformations, Outcomes

The intensive co-creation work resulted in the development of the Air Quality Plan, a binding document for the entire Małopolska Region, with key assumptions and tools for significant ecological changes in the whole region. The Air Quality Plan is a document that, when binding, will regulate issues connected to air pollution in the years to come. In turn, the Kraków Technology Park experts will participate in the assessment of its impact, and attainment of its goals. It is important that the document created will have its effects diligently monitored (Fig. 1).

The prototype of the Air Quality Plan also resulted in the development of an innovative tool: a platform for monitoring industrial pollution to be used by all groups in the commune: for residents to report ecological incidents in their nearest environment, for administration to monitor, prevent and react to such incidents, and for the responsible and conscious enterprises for reporting and documenting potential incidents and emission levels (Figs. 2 and 3).

5 Lessons Learnt and Reflections

The journey of co-creation proved that grassroots initiatives only make sense if properly managed, and following appropriate principles, guidelines, and frameworks. To succeed, it is important to have a good objective, and then co-creative work and appropriately planned processes help to attain it.

The role of the Kraków Technology Park in the process of co-creation of the new Air Quality Plan is worth emphasising. The management of the co-creation process by the KPT, in which extremely different expectations and perspectives were presented, made it possible to maintain objectivism and neutrality of the discussion. To understand the need of the ordinary people of Małopolska, representing smaller municipalities, a few meetings were organised in two small locations near Kraków, with the timing, location, and tools of the workshops adjusted to the expectations of the participants.

The team of the Kraków Technology Park proved high mobilisation, professionalism, and experience in conducting a project of that type. The role of the facilitator and moderator of the co-creation process that the KPT shouldered while co-creating the foundations of the Air Quality Plan proved that there is a huge demand for such an open, innovative, and creative approach at various levels of administration. Working in a group of people with different attitudes and expectations requires an in-depth understanding of the problem, the stakeholders' fears and barriers, to be able to propose non-standard solutions and instruments of support that will help to introduce the much welcome technological improvements in heating sources and environmental policy. The KPT project team was officially introduced into the company structure as the main team dealing with design thinking. Its members continue to improve their qualifications and competences, and the team builds its rich experience on a range of training and consultation projects for various groups of customers.

Running SISCODE project, the team confirmed its leading position of one of two Living Labs in Poland. It is precisely thanks to the experience gathered in that project that the KPT has increased the scope and number of activities of the Living Lab, which has become a significant part of the strategy of the technology park for

a

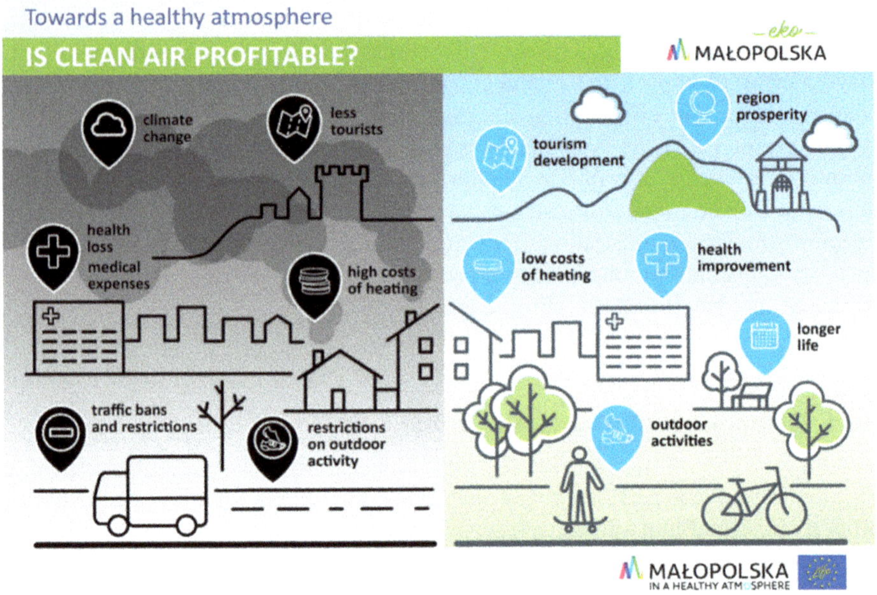

b

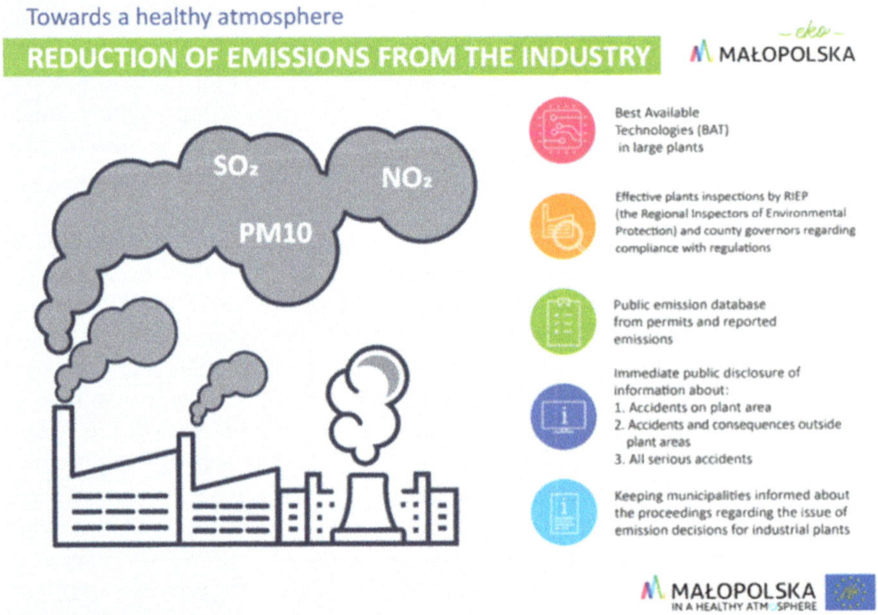

Fig. 1 **a–d** Air protection programme for the Małopolska Region

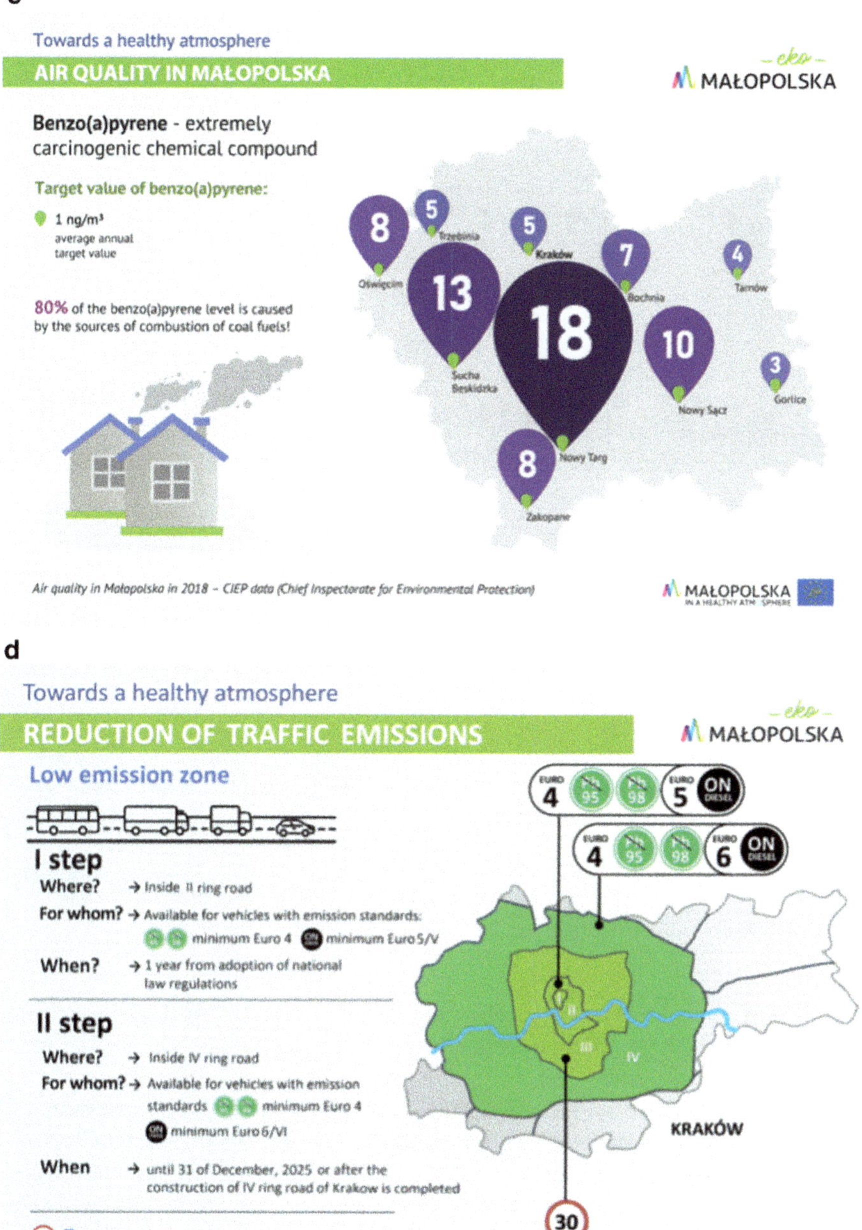

Fig. 1 (continued)

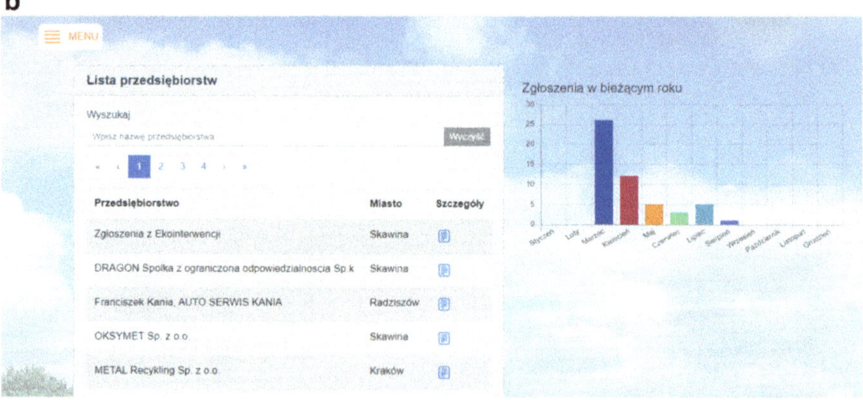

Fig. 2 **a**, **b** Presentation of the platform for the monitoring of industrial pollution

the years to come. Such activities also help the KPT to play a significant role in the developing and driving the economy, and efficiently supporting administration and decision-making groups.

SISCODE and co-creative effort showed the importance of cooperation with multiple customer groups with various needs and requirements on a single project focused on a single goal. It is precisely co-creation that on the one hand allows ordering such consultations in a more extensive group, and on the other elicits the creativity potential from different groups of customers.

The important aspects that, from the start, have accompanied cooperation of the KPT with public administration have been trust, transparency, and openness to new ideas. It is thanks to such a form of cooperation that both the Air Quality Plan for Małopolska Region and the innovative platform for monitoring industrial pollution have become highly successful, and now may be helpful in the years to come.

Fig. 3 The project team, left to right: Monika Machowska, Agnieszka Włodarczyk-Gębik—project coordinator, Aleksandra Gabriel

Work among so many groups proved that each of them also has its internal interests, for example there are often disagreements between administration and business. Similarly, the perspective of looking at the environmental issues among the residents of major cities differs from that of people living in small villages. The case is similar with external factors including financing, human resources, and acts of law that have not always been helpful for the development and progress of work. However, even these obstacles have been a precious experience, as they made it possible to understand and see what elements can be improved, and what can be still tweaked on the path to clean air in the region and in Poland.

An extremely important result of the work was making it possible for the representatives of administration to become familiar with the needs and to listen to the requests of various social groups, which for a variety of reasons they can hardly do in their daily work. Bringing these two groups closer together also inspired such solutions in the future, and encouraged somewhat deeper civil consultations while creating regional policies.

Thanks to SISCODE, stakeholder groups have understood that it is often so that the paths followed are different, yet the goal remains the same. In this case, the goal is clean air not only for today's residents but also for the future generations. Ecological and social changes the team has worked with are idea for whose sake it was worthwhile to employ all the feasible methods of work.

References

1. Air Protection Programme for the Małopolska Region FAQ. https://powietrze.malopolska.pl/en/news/air-protection-programme-for-malopolska-2020-frequently-asked-questions/. Last accessed 2021/03/30
2. KTP Academy. https://www.kpt.Kraków.pl/en/about/akademia-kpt/. Last accessed 2021/03/30
3. KTP. Summary report on co-creation workshops. https://www.kpt.krakow.pl/wp-content/uploads/2019/08/summary-report-on-co-creation-workshops.pdf. Last accessed 2021/03/30
4. Platform for Monitoring Industrial Pollution – Test Version. https://powietrze.malopolska.pl/zanieczyszczenia-przemyslowe/. Last accessed 2021/03/30
5. Traczyk P, Gruszecka-Kosowska A (2020) The condition of air pollution in Kraków, Poland, in 2005–2020, with health risk assessment. Int J Environ Res Public Health 17(17):6063
6. World Health Organization (2009) Protecting health from climate change: connecting science, policy and people

PA4ALL—Innovative Learning Methods for Education in Agriculture: An ICT Based Learning Programme for High Schools

Isidora Stojacic

PA4ALL addresses the topic of introducing precision agriculture tools in high schools specialised in agriculture, exploring the benefits of using the ICT in the field and encouraging high school students to uptake new trends and innovations. The aim is fostering the development of specific skills, greater connection to market needs and relevance for agriculture of the future. Improving the curriculum and fostering the adoption of ICT in schools to a larger scale application, the chapter presents the learning programme that scientists, trainers, and policymakers co-designed aiming at long term benefits to agriculture production and the labour market in Serbia.

1 Introduction

The case study of *PA4ALL* in the SISCODE project gathers the aforementioned in one scope. After conducting the interviews with the relevant actors, the team understood that the curriculum in high schools specialised in agriculture does not support the subjects related to ICT in general, nor do the school facility infrastructures support the implementation of ICT. Also, despite recent increase in the number of young people engaged in agriculture, Serbia still lags behind the countries in Europe. In the European Union, young farmers account for 8% of the total number of agricultural producers. In the Czech Republic and Poland, this percentage is even higher. In Serbia, however, less than 5 percent of young people are engaged in agriculture. By implementing precision agriculture tools into high school mandatory curriculum, *PA4ALL* together with BioSense will be able to achieve its long-term goal. Therefore, it can be said that the best solution for us to follow in SISCODE was the introduction of ICT subjects in agriculture courses, inclusion of ICT in

I. Stojacic (✉)
BioSense Institute, University of Novi Sad, Novi Sad, Serbia

© The Author(s) 2022

A. Deserti et al. (eds.), *Co-creation for Responsible Research and Innovation*,
Springer Series in Design and Innovation 15,
https://doi.org/10.1007/978-3-030-78733-2_8

schools specialised in agriculture, increase the awareness of the relationship between technology and agriculture.

2   Ecosystem, Context and Challenge Addressed

PA4ALL is an abbreviation for Precision Agriculture for All, which is also the main scope of the Living Lab, to introduce all the actors in the agriculture production chain to precision agriculture tools. The host organisation of *PA4ALL* is BioSense Institute [1], Institute for research and development of information technology in biosystems. Research and innovation at BioSense Institute is developed in a close interaction with farmers and the agrifood sector, government bodies, entrepreneurs and business community, international researchers, and citizens. BioSense collaborates to create a new generation of open innovations which will be readily used and which will bring benefits across the entire value-chain. As a meeting place for all relevant stakeholders, *PA4ALL* was established—the Living Lab for precision agriculture. This is the first Living Laboratory in Serbia and the first one in Europe to focus on precision agriculture. *PA4ALL* takes full advantage of inter-sectoral cross-fertilisation of ideas and offers possibilities to test ideas and prototypes in the real-world setting.

PA4ALL is located in Novi Sad, Serbia and is the only institution in the region focused on the topic of ICT in the agri-food sector. BioSense advances and integrates all that ICT can offer today—nanomaterials, low-cost miniature sensors, satellite imaging, robotics, big data analytics—to provide as much information as possible to the agricultural sector. The final goal of BioSense is to incorporate all efforts and results of various research groups into a unique BioSense integrated system for agricultural monitoring. This system will provide necessary data sets and create breakthroughs in the agrifood sector, not only in terms of increased efficiency, reduced pollution and monetary savings, but also in the way that farming is perceived and performed, making agriculture acceptable as a career choice to younger generations of farmers.

Co-creation represents a crucial method with all its tools for *PA4ALL*, since the Lab requires constant communication and feedback with the actors in the industry in order to facilitate the adoption of ICT in agriculture. Therefore, *PA4ALL* has its own ecosystem of farmers, SMEs operating in the field of agriculture, policymakers, schools specialised in agriculture where co-creation enables efficient interaction.

Ecosystem and context

The political context in Serbia in the past decades had brought a lot of turbulence to the society followed by frequent changes in relevant governmental institutions. Furthermore, as a society in transition, Serbia is facing the challenge of keeping up with the global challenges lacking the necessary technology and industry that would enable this process. However, previous socialist legacy provides Serbia with quality education in engineering professions, primarily electronics and mechanical engineering, It is exactly these fields that have in recent years become the pioneers of change influencing both policy and market and bringing ICT to the forefront of Serbia's export potential, talent pool and educational opportunities. A recent study conducted by the German-Serbian Chamber of commerce confirms that ICT is the fastest growing sector in the Serbian economy.

Given these developments, local policy context has also been changing. Traditionally, the lack of democratic institutions has led to a lack of bottom-up initiatives and little understanding for the co-creation process when talking about new initiatives and changes in the system. However, the growing potential of the ICT sector has led to the development of organisations and institutions with a common goal of working towards changing the institutional framework to increase the potential of the sector. ICT Clusters representing a group of companies, SMEs or start-ups formed in cities such as Novi Sad, Subotica, Nis, Belgrade and many others. Digital Serbia Initiative brings together banks, media companies, ICT companies, phone operators and acts in their best interest working on necessary policy changes.

In agriculture, more traditional approaches to policy are deployed. Most farmers form cooperatives and use these structures to influence crop prices, gain greater bargaining power when negotiating with the state, influence subventions etc. In this field, compared to ICT, serious co-creation and bottom-up policy initiatives have not yet happened.

As *PA4ALL* works at the intersection of the two respective fields, the assessment of the policy context through initial desk research as well as previous presence in the community directed us towards working more through the ICT community. Capitalizing on the current digital strategies, bottom-up initiatives and potential of ICT for Serbia's development, focusing the policy efforts here.

BioSense Institute is involved in multidisciplinary research performed in the fields of micro and nanoelectronics, communications, signal processing, remote sensing, big data, robotics and biosystems the team consulted the research groups on what kind of help can be provided to high schools specialised in agriculture in order to prepare its students for the future labor market. Remote sensing and GIS group gave us an excellent reference on which equipment should be provided to schools in order to help them learn more about the popular concept of Big Data analysis, which could be applied to agriculture as well. Since this group bases its research on processing, storage and retrieval of data acquired from multimodal sensors, and integration of large amounts of multimodal data acquired from different sources, the idea of organising training in high schools was born. The activities of the group include the development of systems for instant access to relevant data presented in ways which are the most informative to end users, such as GIS databases, which could be interesting to future professionals in agriculture.

Challenge

Farmers can no longer rely on timeworn coping strategies when all of their familiar benchmarks for making agricultural decisions are becoming increasingly less reliable. This raises the need for additional means such as ICT technologies applied in the field of agriculture. Many ICT in agriculture or digital agriculture interventions have been developed and tested around the world to help agriculturists improve their livelihoods through increased agricultural productivity and income, or by reducing risks.

PA4ALL started by introducing precision agriculture tools in high schools specialised in agriculture by presenting the benefits of using the ICT in agriculture and encouraging high school students to uptake new trends and innovations. After conducting desk research and interviews during the co-creation process with the stakeholders, *PA4ALL* concluded that the best solution would be to provide meteostations to one selected school, which will provide the best innovation idea related to ICT in agriculture. The meteostations will provide information such as soil humidity, air temperature, precipitation amounts, air humidity, wind direction through the BioSense internal platform—AgroSense which provides various data on personalised agriculture production. The final aim was to improve the curriculum in schools with this new module and change the adoption of ICT in schools on a larger scale, considering the notion that the younger agricultural household members are a demographic group that has demonstrated higher adoption rates of technology.

PA4ALL focuses on connecting the citizens and the policymakers in order to incorporate the whole co-creation process. As *PA4ALL* works at the intersection of two fields, ICT and agriculture, the assessment of the policy context through initial desk research as well as previous presence in the community directed the team towards interacting more with some ICT community bodies using co-creation tools. The existing governmental strategies which are addressing the current policies that incentivise the implementation of ICT in education in Serbia (Digital Agenda) one could expect more innovation and mind set changes on a society level. Directly, co-creation activities brought positive examples to the policymakers on how the curriculum in schools could be improved and how the society could react to such educational system reforms. These encounters and moments of exchange took place during workshops, events, presentations, fair exhibitions and other events prepared for the local, regional and national policymakers involved in the project. Therefore, this initiated a set of indirect benefits such as digitalisation on a larger scale, not only in agriculture. Furthermore, by adding courses related to information technology to regular school curriculums encouraging children to understand the impact ICT has in various spheres not only in ones already known to them. It was possible to demonstrate that fields such as agriculture, industry, traffic, tourism and other branches of the economy benefit greatly from ICT and bring economic growth to individuals as well.

3 The Co-creation Journey

Context analysis

The Desk Research was undertaken in order to identify the crucial aspects lacking in the educational systems of Serbia related to ICT and agriculture. As aforementioned, firstly, materials used for this research were documents on Digital Strategy of Serbia and Strategy of development of information society in Serbia 2020. Furthermore, desk research uncovered existing initiatives promoting ICT education in schools and helped in developing next steps for conducting interviews.

Secondly, one school was selected as a reference point. Interviews were conducted with teacher Branislav Jovanovic and his students from a high school specialised in agriculture in Futog. The main questions addressed were related to their professional specialisation, additional workshops and seminars, training on ICT in agriculture and new equipment. After further analysing their needs, *PA4ALL* better understood the urgency of implementing ICT in the educational system of Serbia.

Finally, *PA4ALL* reached its network of innovators such as farmers, small and medium enterprises (SME's) and entrepreneurs, and asked them to provide their professional opinions on how schools specialised in agriculture could better address the current needs of the market and create better professionals in the field.

Problem framing

The analysed data helped to determine what are the crucial needs of schools to develop their curriculum activities and introduce new aspects in agriculture education.

The first established contact with schools around Serbia was at the Science Festival at the University of Novi Sad. The aim was to welcome the students attending schools specialised in agriculture to provide their ideas on new prototypes which could be developed, and which would help in solving some of the issues related to agriculture. After the ideas were presented at the science festival, which took place from May 18th until May 19th 2019, the best idea was selected and awarded with equipment which will bring ICT closer to students. The idea selected was called "SPRAYCONDI—a digital advisor for the reduction of errors in the application of pesticides' suggested by the high school specialised in agriculture from Futog, located in the suburbs of Novi Sad. "SPRAYCONDI" would help the farmer make the right decision regarding the reduction of drift and more efficient pesticide application, measurement of meteorological data at the site where the pesticide application is performed. The digitised data would also be transmitted via mobile network to a cloud or computer where a model for the impact of the pesticide application on biomass and the final yield will be generated. This data was supposed to be obtained at the meteorological stations on a regional level, which is why it has been decided to provide the meteostations to schools, so they could obtain the data locally form their own sources.

The idea provided by the school in Futog was evaluated as highly innovative and exactly the right way of thinking that was aimed to be induced in the heads of high-school children. The teacher who was working together with the team on this project was delighted to hear that the project will actually bring practical results to the school and that the children will be able to not only think of an idea but also be able to see how precision agriculture actually works in real life.

Envisioning solutions

The farmers community around BioSense provided information on activities which are necessary in order to improve the ICT-based knowledge inside the farmers community in Serbia in general. During the Annual ANTARES Workshop which took place from April 3rd until April 5th 2019., AgroSense—BioSense's platform was presented together with its main services designed for farmers who were invited to the workshop. The opportunity was taken to consult the farmers as users and other stakeholders regarding the plans for the SISCODE project and the idea of improving the educational system in agricultural specialised schools was strongly supported. The farmers provided advice on how to structure ideas regarding the needed equipment, how to address the students and it was pointed out how important it is for young professionals in the agricultural sector to use novel technologies such as the AgroSense platform, Big Data from meteostations, and others.

An additional source of information about the needed activities in schools which will improve the education of future professionals in the AgTech industry was the BioSense network, which comprises SMEs and start-ups. Since most of the entrepreneurs belonging to the network have a background in agriculture and ICT related sciences, they were an excellent reference point to suggest relevant changes and new ideas regarding the educational system. Since BIOS Institute is also involved in multidisciplinary research performed in the fields of micro and nanoelectronics, communications, signal processing, remote sensing, big data, robotics and biosystems consulting the research groups on what kind of help can be provided to high schools specialised in agriculture in order to prepare its students for the future labor market.

It was of crucial importance to gather ideas and info from experts who were already operating in the field of precision agriculture, both the end-users and the actual developers of the technologies. These actors were a perfect example of how two worlds would be combined, the ones who were the creator -researchers and the ones who were in the position to give complaints, suggest changes, innovations, and underline problems which occur in real life settings.

Developing and prototyping

In order to prototype the educational model designed by *PA4ALL* (BioSense Institute) a meteo station was installed on a piece of land in Futog, the city where *PA4ALL* (BioSense Institute) is located. The meteostation is now part of the agriculture equipment in the high school specialised in agriculture in Futog which enables the teachers and students to use precision agriculture tools themselves. Apart from installing the meteo station *PA4ALL* provided additional equipment such as laptops, video projectors and printers in order to help the school collect and manipulate meteorological data from the stations. *PA4ALL* also provided credentials to this high school digital platform AgroSense to allow them to evaluate the data such as precipitation, air or soil temperature. Finally, Vladan Minić, a researcher from *PA4ALL* explained to the teachers how to use AgroSense and demonstrated its benefits for agriculture production. The teachers and students showed deep interest in new technologies and in this educational model since they are aware of the necessity to improve the curriculum in schools by introducing precision agriculture as one of the subjects. They also understand that traditional agriculture production is a matter of the past and that precision agriculture is the future.

The policy officials underlined the main issue with this specific focus group, which is the fact that agriculture is not an interesting field for young people and that ICT can change the perception that young people have on agriculture - a crucial sector for any economy. Furthermore, the benefits of co-creation tools have been exploited in order to gather feedback and raise interest for our initiative. At the moment, an active dialogue with the responsible bodies is ongoing with the aim of paving the way for the necessary changes in the educational system and therefore improving the high school curriculum.

4 Experimentation: Output, Transformations, Outcomes

Final concept

The main solution offered in the SISCODE project is the new model design which could be implemented in high school curriculum on a national level and therefore would be applied in every school around Serbia. The services of AgroSense will be useful to schools since they will be able to see how a similar technology looks in practice. AgroSense has an option of mapping the parameters of the farm, with an option by which the images from the drones can be placed on the desired production plot, the maps of the conductivity of the soil obtained by the electro-magnetic probe, the yield maps of the combine and any other georeferenced images. By applying all these functions in a real context, our new learning module can be structured according to teachers and students identified needs and interests.

It is also important to mention that the formal and semi-formal bodies who focus on lobbying for advancement in ICT have been formed in recent years. This will support the sustainability of the project in the long run, since Serbia is heading towards a more digitised economy.

Co-creation tools were used when face-to-face meetings with the school directors during the meeting organised annually by the Ministry of Education where they discuss current issues and potential collaborations between schools. *PA4ALL* attended last year's meeting when the project initiative and the final goal was presented. The project idea came to be a source of appreciation from the school directors' side towards the organisation which made the working group proud and consider the next steps to be done. In the context of ensuring the project sustainability led to an idea to look for additional funds—national ones, which would help in suppling other schools, not only the one where the final solution was prototyped, with additional meteostations. Finally having succeeded in this activity at the moment it is aimed to implement the initial idea and install the new meteostations in other 8 schools around Serbia.

Transformations triggered

The *PA4ALL* team learned that co-creation in science withholds the potential for long-term positive results. Through co-creation the future potential of agriculture in Serbia can be shaped, just by interconnecting different important stakeholders. On an individual level co-creating can facilitate scientific research by providing precise directions and insights on a specific topic from an individual or organisation who is already involved in it. The flow of information is facilitated, lack of experiences does not impose a threat. On an organisational level, co-creating brings synergy, better organisational structure and deep engagement of the actors. *PA4ALL* understood that co-creating can bring together stakeholders from different levels of administration, therefore it could improve policies on city, region and even country level.

Recently, because of the COVID-19 situation, *PA4ALL* strives to engage the students using social media and online communication platforms such as Zoom or GoToMeeting, however since the schools were completely closed the case structure needed to be reorganised a bit.

5   Lessons Learnt and Reflections

PA4ALL detected that agriculture is significantly dropping in the numbers of people employed. Also, when compared to other high schools, those specialised in agriculture attract only 6% of yearly applicants, while grammary school enrolment is 26%, IT schools' enrolment 11% and economic/law high schools' enrolment is 13%. This is why it is aimed to make agriculture appealing for the youth of Serbia again. It has been directly demonstrated how precision agriculture tools can be used in the field and by promoting the use of advanced ICT solutions to high school children, they were enabled to adopt the use of precision agriculture in their own family agriculture production.

Additionally, it is planned to conduct other workshops with students and with teachers, which will be an extra activity aimed at the sustainability of the case study. It is planned to organise a summer school which will be linked to another project DATADRAGON[1] where high school children from all around Serbia will be able to learn more and try to use other precision agriculture tools such as robotic platforms, etc. [2]. Since the COVID-19 situation is in place at the moment there are some difficulties organising the events, but they are definitely in place for the future. Datadragon organises hackathons and events where people around the world come to learn more about Big Data in Agriculture and Precision Agriculture tools on a large scale.

Finally, when speaking about sustainability, it can be said that one of our main achievements is getting funds from national projects which will fund the meteo-stations being supplied to various schools around Serbia, which is already taking place as we speak, so other schools, not just the one in Futog will be able to use the model and the designed curriculum. More importantly, it will be able to influence more children to adopt precision agriculture tools. In addition, what marked this case study was the actual application of co-creation practices for the purpose of achieving the final goal. Throughout the entire course of the project various co-creation tools were applied such as interaction platforms, feedback gathering forms, various experimenting tools with the actors in the project, etc. All of the processes

---

[1] https://datadragon.eu/.

used were designed by the team as well as the entire process in order to finalise the scope and change the curriculum, and was designed together with the school and the organisation's own community.

References

1. BioSens Institute. https://biosens.rs/. Last accessed 2021/03/12
2. Datadragon. https://datadragon.eu/. Last accessed 2021/03/12

ThessAHALL—A Life-Long Learning Programme for the Social Inclusion of "Early-Stage" Older Adult Researchers

Despoina Mantziari, Evdokimos Konstantinidis, Despoina Petsani, Nikolaos Kyriakidis, Vassiliki Zilidou, Efstathios Sidiropoulos, Maria Nikolaidou, Aikaterini-Marina Katsouli, and Panagiotis Bamidis

Aiming at limiting the risk of ageism and social exclusion of older adults in society, the Thessaloniki Acive & Healthy Ageing Living Lab (*Thess-AHALL*) looks at co-design and open science solutions for social inclusion for the ageing population. The chapter presents the "Partners of Experience", a participatory life-long learning programme, consisting of a series of co-creation research and experiential learning activities in the Thess-AHALL Living Lab, part of the Medical Physics Lab, School of Medicine of the Aristotle University of Thessaloniki (AUTH), and the City of

D. Mantziari · E. Konstantinidis · D. Petsani · N. Kyriakidis · V. Zilidou · E. Sidiropoulos · M. Nikolaidou · A.-M. Katsouli · P. Bamidis (✉)
Laboratory of Medical Physics and Digital Innovation, School of Medicine, Faculty of Health Sciences, Aristotle University of Thessaloniki, Thessaloniki, Greece
e-mail: bamidis@auth.gr

Thessaloniki Active and Healthy Ageing Living Lab (Thess-AHALL), Thessaloniki, Greece

D. Mantziari
e-mail: mantziad@auth.gr

E. Konstantinidis
e-mail: evdokimosk@auth.gr

D. Petsani
e-mail: petsanid@auth.gr

V. Zilidou
e-mail: vizilidou@auth.gr

E. Sidiropoulos
e-mail: stathsid@auth.gr

M. Nikolaidou
e-mail: mnikola@auth.gr

A.-M. Katsouli
e-mail: katsoulia@auth.gr

A. Deserti et al. (eds.), *Co-creation for Responsible Research and Innovation*, Springer Series in Design and Innovation 15, https://doi.org/10.1007/978-3-030-78733-2_9

Thessaloniki that encourage cooperation between older adults and the R&D scientific community of the University.

1 Introduction

For over a decade, the Thessaloniki Active and Healthy Aging Living Lab (*Thess-AHALL*) fosters research initiatives pursuing co-creation and social innovation. Its aim is to improve the physical, mental and social health as well as care processes of older adults and other vulnerable populations like chronic patients. This is done by encouraging regional development and sustainability of novel technologies in the Active and Healthy Ageing (AHA) domain. **Within the SISCODE context, the *Thess-AHALL* has aimed to tackle the risk of social exclusion in relation to ageism and enhance the active citizenship of older adults, deploying an innovative participatory and experiential life-long learning programme for early-stage researchers over 65 years old, the so-called "Partners of Experience".**

Thess-AHALL's long-standing experience in collaborating with the targeted population has shown that older adults often experience social marginalisation and the cultural stigma of losing their mental and physical abilities due to health problems or ageing [1–3]. At the same time, although science and research have a high impact on society, the scientific community is still seen as a "close elite" that does not address and reflect on citizens' real needs. Taking these two aspects into account, the *Thess-AHALL* launched the "Partners of Experience" life-long learning programme with the aim to open the university and the environment of research for society embracing citizens. Older adults are involved specifically in the described case promoting the equal and mutual collaboration from both sides to foster social innovation and the co-design of solutions for everyday living challenges.

The concept is based on the perception that a more inclusive approach from the scientific community actively involving society could become a vehicle for vulnerable populations to tackle stigmatisation and enhance social skills and competences, while addressing effectively everyday living key societal problems in collaboration with policymakers and experts [6]. In this framework, a total number of 44 older adult early-stage researchers, members of the "Collaboration and Research Community for Independent Living", powered by AUTH Medical Physics Lab, attended the "Partners of Experience" programme for a whole academic year exploiting applied scientific research & co-creation methodologies. A concrete concept model of the proposed life-long learning programme has been the outcome of this experiential co-creation journey, aspiring to be replicated and further exploited in similar and diverse contexts in the future.

2 Ecosystem, Context and Challenge Addressed

The absence of a horizontal national policy framework towards ageism has led to unequal access to the benefits of social inclusion activities for the target population across Greece, as the implementation of social inclusion policies for older adults is at the discretion of the municipal and regional authorities. More specifically, the local municipal authorities are responsible for providing educational programmes for older adults (e.g. teaching computers skills, foreign languages etc.), entertaining and cultural activities (e.g. dance classes, physical exercise programmes, ageing tourism etc.) as well as operating the local day care and activity centres. On the other hand, there are remarkable, although fragmentary, initiatives, undertaken by individual organisations or other types of local policymaking actors: e.g. private companies, the National Health Districts, NGOs, Patients' associations, universities etc., either as part of their action plans for the ageing population or as part of their Corporate Social Responsibility (CSR) commitments, including soft-skills training seminars for older adults or programmes for the employment of older people.

Within this framework, and thanks to its many-year experience in research in the field of Active and Healthy Aging (AHA), the *Thess-AHALL* has established its own action plan, often exploiting social innovation and open science initiatives or awareness raising activities. One example for this are the Play4/Participate4 common cause campaigns that entail lectures open to the public, participatory & experiential research activities, etc., in a way to promote the openness of the scientific community to the society [6]. Furthermore, it aims at the engagement and close collaboration of researchers, policymakers, experts and citizens (the Quadruple Helix) as a means for effectively addressing key societal challenges in the fields of Health and Well-Being.

The actual strength of *Thess-AHALL* lies in its wide network of collaborators within the Quadruple Helix at the local, national and EU levels -i.e. academic partners, municipalities, healthcare authorities, hospitals, care centres, NGOs, SMEs, healthcare professionals and experts, as well as its own Community of older adult researchers [7]. It constantly promotes the active engagement of all the interested parties in every step of the development of a new solution or initiative (Agile Development Methodology) [4, 5]. *Thess-AHALL's* national and international synergies, its involvement in a wide number of research projects in the AHA domain as well as the deep knowledge and the high expertise of its researchers, working with older adults for over a decade have resulted in extensive capacities in the fields of Responsible Research and Social Innovation. This knowledge enables the transfer of know-how and the generation of social change in the local ecosystem.

Considering this starting point, the *Thess-AHALL* launched the "Partners of Experience" life-long learning programme with one main objective: to fight the downsides of ageism and enhance the active citizenship of older adult and outpatient population by bridging the gap among citizens, researchers and policymakers by uniting them with the common goal of collaboratively addressing everyday living problems of society. To achieve this, the *Thess-AHALL* applies its existing knowledge on co-creation and citizen science principles to open the university to society and obtain a change in the established perception that academia still remains a separated elite section of society detached from its real needs. In this context, the *Thess-AHALL* welcomes older population back to the community and re-introduces them as an alternative, experiential research group that applies step-by-step scientific & co-creation research methodologies to design and implement solutions **for and with society** [6].

3 The Co-creation Journey

To enhance its pre-existing empirical knowledge of working with the targeted population and identify solid ground for exploring its challenge, the *Thess-AHALL* followed a four-step co-creation journey with older adults as its primary beneficiaries and involving all the interested stakeholders as policymakers, researchers and experts. This journey, proposed as a general framework within the SISCODE project was tested and validated by the 10 co-creation labs described in this volume following the steps of (i) the context analysis of the challenge to be addressed, (ii) the reframing of the problem, (iii) the envisioning of alternative solutions and (iv) the prototyping of the most prevalent solution.

In the framework of the context analysis, the *Thess-AHALL* conducted an in-depth desk research, as well as a number of interviews and focus groups with interested stakeholders to collect both quantitative and qualitative data on the impact of ageism on older adults social health and life, as well as the "openness" of academia. The desk research provided valuable information on the raised research questions confirming the experiential knowledge and initial assumptions of the *Thess-AHALL*. Interviews with healthcare professionals sealed the findings of the desk research in relation to the crucial role of inclusive activities for the targeted population social health and their active involvement in society. Finally, a series of interviews and focus groups with older adults (the Collaboration and Research Community for Independent Living and the Parkinson's Association of Northern Greece) showed that previous experiences of participatory activities in the Living Lab had improved participants' sense of social acceptance and active citizenship, as well as their sense of belonging to a group. Members perceived themselves as equal contributors who can share their thoughts and needs and actively be part of the design of new solutions [7, 8].

The collected feedback from the interviews and focus groups strengthened the Living Lab's vision to apply participatory activities to address its challenge, while it also contributed to the reframing of the initially defined problem. Specifically, *Thess-AHALL's* first proposition was to fight the downsides of ageism by introducing the "Participate 4" common cause campaigns: Older adults and chronic patients should be motivated to gamify their participation in social awareness actions and co-creation activities with and for other' vulnerable populations and donate their time to be turned into a symbolic offer (tangible or intangible) accredited to a joint, predetermined cause. Despite receiving positive remarks for the innovative approach to raise awareness, both experts and the targeted stakeholders raised their concerns on the campaigns' sustainability, mainly related the limited participation in such actions, highlighting the need for a concrete solution, primarily orientated at the direct benefits for the targeted population (i.e. older adults' needs and expectations) [6].

This affirmation led to the development iteration of the very first solution. Once again, it was the input from interviews with older adults, expressing their satisfaction for participating in Living Lab's activities, that helped researchers to envision the new solution of setting up a "learning-by-doing" process, emphasising on the potential value of their active involvement in participatory research and the implementation of solutions for "them" and for "their society". As an interactive and highly-engaging solution was sought, based on the principles of co-creation and RRI, a new research question was raised: **"What if instead of an older-adult-student group, there was an older-adult-early-stage-research group?"** Beneficiaries would have the opportunity to learn and enhance their active participation in the society by experientially applying the scientific research methodology or in other words "being in the shoes of a *Thess-AHALL* researchers", working for a whole academic year as mutual collaborators of the Living Lab, not just attendees, to solve everyday life's problems of their interest. And that was when the "Partners of Experience" initiative was officially born!

4　Experimentation: Output, Transformations, Outcomes

The "Partners of Experience" solution was introduced as a life-long, experiential research programme to address everyday living challenges of older adult early-stage researchers and their peers. For a whole academic year, the 44 older adults involved the programme tested and validated the proposed life-long learning activities, divided in three smaller, thematic research groups (Environment—Health & Social Welfare—Active Citizenship) guided by the *Thess-AHALL* researchers. Over the duration of nine months, the prototyping (Sept 2019–Jun 2020) took place with the three groups that closely collaborated with local policymakers, healthcare professionals and the scientific community, applying step-by-step the scientific research methodology, adjusted to a more experiential learning way. This was aimed to explore and implement solutions for making Thessaloniki a healthier and more accessible city for older adults. The "Partners of Experience" life-long learning programme included a series of 12 activities: Eight of them were conducted as face-to-face sessions between September 2019 and February 2020, while the rest of them went virtually, via Skype/Viber and phone group calls, due to the COVID-19 restrictions. The in-person activities comprised the 1st loop of the prototyping phase including activities primarily related to the first four steps of the proposed methodology arriving at initial considerations for the implementation of solutions. The virtual sessions composed the 2nd loop and consequently the final stage of solutions' implementation, dissemination and final evaluation of the programme (Fig. 1).

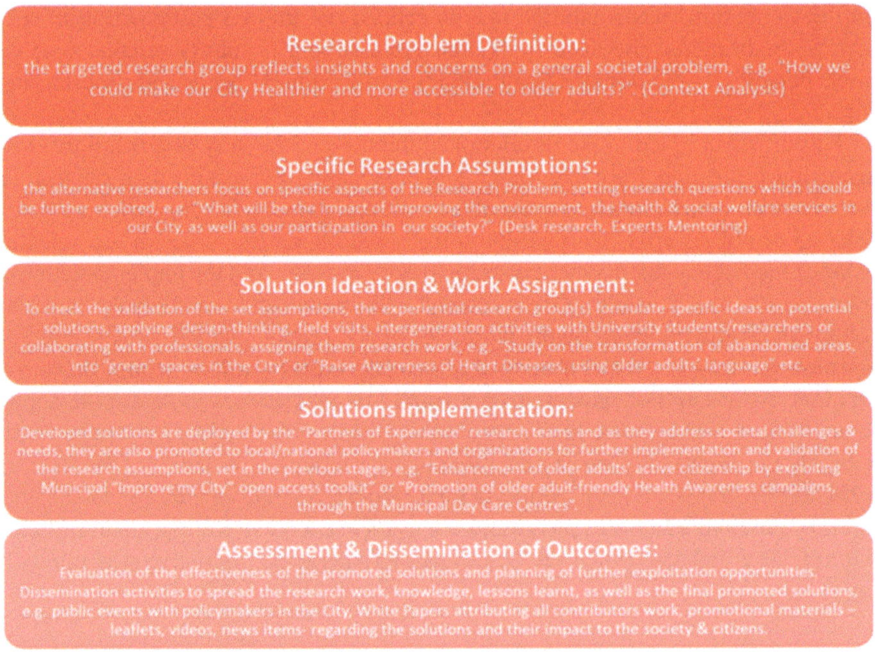

Fig. 1 The "Partners of Experience" methodology steps, followed by the participants of the programme

During the prototyping, older adult researchers tested and evaluated the proposed programme, which is summarised in the following experiential and co-creation activities:

- **Public deliberation and panel sessions** to create an agenda and define the programme's priorities in a co-setting (until Sept 2019)
- **Design-thinking and ideation sessions** for the approval of the proposed activities and the selection of Thematic Research Areas (Sept–Nov 2019)
- **Desk research** in the AUTH University Library and online sources during hands-on workshops (Dec 2019)
- **Field visits** in the university premises and the city for the confirmation of the research hypothesis and to brainstorm on solutions (Oct 2019–Mar 2020)
- **Intergenerational lectures and collaboration with post-graduate students** in assignments of their semester work (Nov 2019–Dec 2020)
- **Mentoring sessions with experts and policymakers** to select the final solution from the proposed ideas for implementation (Nov 2019–Dec 2020)
- **Online group sessions**—due to the COVID-19 restrictions (Mar 2020–Jun 2020)
- **"Home" assignments** for the design and implementation of the solutions as well as their final evaluation and assessment of the programme (June 2020).

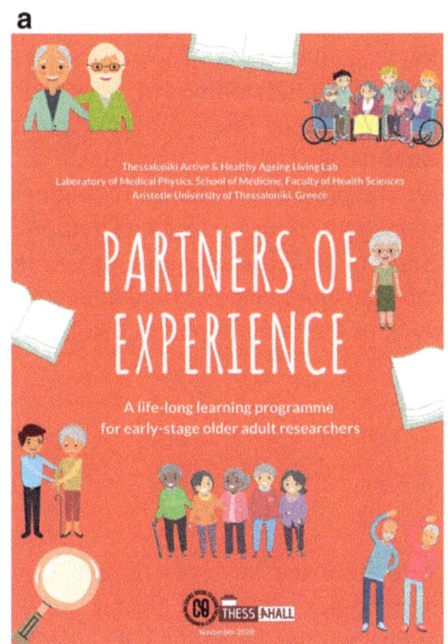

Thess-AHALL's many-year experience in collaborating with the targeted populations has shown that they often feel socially marginalized, facing the cultural stigma of losing their mental and physical abilities, due to health problems or ageing. At the same time, although science has a high impact for societies, the scientific community is still seen as a "close elite", not addressing citizens' real needs. Taking these into account, **Thess-AHALL's "Partners of Experience" programme "opens the Academia's door" to the society and embraces older adults, as an alternative research group, who co-creates solutions for everyday living challenges.**

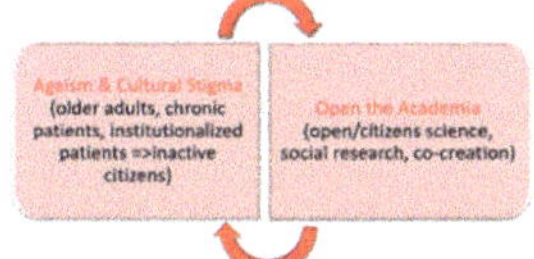

The challenge aims to prove that a more accessible scientific community with the high involvement of citizens in participatory research and decision-making, could become the solid ground for targeted populations to tackle potential stigmatization, as well as for societies to address effectively key societal problems with the assent and mutual collaboration of citizens and experts.

In this framework, **a total number of 44 older adult early-stage researchers attended the "Partners of Experience" programme for a whole academic year (September 2019-June 2020)**, applying scientific research methodology, either in Face-to-Face sessions or virtually (CoVid-19 pandemic). Split in three smaller research groups and guided by Thess-AHALL "mentors", participants addressed equal societal challenges, regarding Environment – Health & Social Welfare – Active Citizenship topics, to make the city of Thessaloniki "healthier" and more accessible to peers.

Fig. 2 **a**, **b** Preview of the "Partners of Experience" methodology handbook

The whole methodology, its activities and lessons learned from this first cycle of the programme have been included in a practical guide, a step-by-step handbook, accessible to anyone interested to explore the methodology (Fig. 2 a, b).

From its very first activities, the "Partners of Experience" programme received positive comments from all the involved stakeholders, especially stressing the programme's positive impact on the social inclusion and acceptance, as well as the high engagement of its beneficiaries who asked for its replication to address more societal problems in the future. At the same time, the local ecosystem has also been remarkably affected by the pilot *Thess-AHALL* has conducted within the SISCODE project. Local policymakers, i.e. the Municipality of Thessaloniki and the Region of Central Macedonia, as supporters of the "Partners of Experience" programme, are willing to embrace the programme or part of its activities in their future action plans for older adults as soon as the pandemic comes to its end. Moreover, the close collaboration between older adults, researchers and policymakers, aiming to bridge the gap between the city and its citizens as well as among the citizens, highlighted the importance of collaboration of all the interested parts within a society for solving key societal issues. In addition to this, the members of the research community who were involved in the process, and especially the postgraduate students participating in the intergenerational activities, recognised that the experiential knowledge of citizens is a valuable resource for science to avoid developing solutions that do not fit to the community's needs and they have become more open to embrace or lead similar initiatives in the future.

In the meantime, the "Partners of Experience" programme equipped the *Thess-AHALL* with new knowledge and skills for the systematisation of the co-creation activities in the Living Lab. The exploitation of the SISCODE toolbox in every phase of the co-creation journey and the deployment of prototype phase of the "Partners of Experience" programme, have been emblematic case studies of the transformation achieved within the organisation. Moreover, the project's challenge highlighted the importance of maintaining stakeholders' engagement in a more concrete way and establishing a framework on the sustainability of such a community. It was the SISCODE project which led *Thess-AHALL* to the development and implementation of their own panel management tool to keep track of the logistics, participation and ethics of its stakeholders.

5 Lessons Learnt and Reflections

In conclusion, the *Thess-AHALL* has chosen to fight the key societal challenge related to social, mental health and well-being of older adults and chronic outpatients being at risk of ageism and cultural stigma within the SISCODE context,. The barriers identified during the 1st loop of prototyping were carefully considered during the pivoting phase and resulted in an updated plan. The co-creation process and the continuous communication with the community of stakeholders enabled the programme to advance and transform into the final prototype presented above. *Thess-AHALL* has already investigated future directions for exploiting the programme in other institutions and specific conversations are ongoing with the Municipality of Thessaloniki and the "Archangelos Michail" nursing home in Nicosia, Cyprus for a future implementation of the programme. However, the COVID-19 pandemic has delayed the procedures and plans significantly.

Moreover, regarding the involvement of policymakers, the Living Lab has adopted new approaches in addressing and engaging policymakers from different levels in various stages of the co-creation process. As it has already been mentioned, the SISCODE project and the "Partners of Experience" programme provided the opportunity to the *Thess-AHALL* to establish and adopt a specific strategy for stakeholder engagement and systematise plenty of its activities related to co-creation and citizens' science. Moreover, the COVID-19 situation lead to the materialisation of the need for alternative means of communication, engagement and collaboration with stakeholders, especially older adults, who are low digitally skilled and cannot use virtual means.

Furthermore, the *Thess-AHALL* pilot highlighted the importance of co-creation and user involvement in the field of research for older adult's health and wellbeing. Older people usually are left out of the research developments, increasing the risks of manifestation of the downsides of ageism like social exclusion. At *Thess-AHALL*, the core team believes that their participation in the research can assist in the development of more concrete and user-friendly solutions and additionally be beneficial for their own social life and wellbeing.

References

1. Cantarella A, Borella E, Carretti B, Kliegel M, de Beni R (2017) Benefits in tasks related to everyday life competences after a working memory training in older adults. Int J Geriatr Psychiatry 32(1):86–93
2. Maffoni M, Giardini A, Pierobon A, Ferrazzoli D, Frazzitta G (2017) Stigma experienced by Parkinson's disease patients: a descriptive review of qualitative studies. Parkinson's Dis 2017
3. Kaushansky L, Boudreau D, Keirns C (2016) Is there a doctor in the house? Students explore home, history, and the evolution of medicine. J Mus Educ 41(1):52–58
4. Petsani D, Evdokimos K, Billis A, Tessarolo F, Anzivino S, Nollo G, Conotter V, Onorati G (2018) SISCODE deliverable D7.3—pilot trials in living labs methodology
5. Tessarolo F, Nollo G, Conotter V, Onorati G, Konstantinidis EI, Petsani D, Bamidis PD (2019) User-centered co-design and AGILE methodology for developing ambient assisting technologies: study plan and methodological framework of the CAPTAIN project. In: 2019 IEEE 23rd International symposium on consumer technologies, ISCT 2019
6. Mantziari DA, Petsani DG, Konstantinidis EI (2019) Ageism and open Academia: exploring new pathways towards the limitation of social exclusion of older adults and chronic patients. In: Oral presentation at the European triple helix congress on responsible innovation & entrepreneurship (ETHAC2019), Thessaloniki, Greece, 30 September–1 October 2019
7. Konstantinidis EI, Billis A, Bratsas C et al (2016) Thessaloniki active and healthy ageing living lab: the roadmap from a specific project to a living lab towards openness. In: PETRA '16: proceedings of the 9th ACM international conference on PErvasive technologies related to assistive environments, Corfu Island, Greece, June 2016, Article No.: 73, pp.1–4. New York, NY, United States: Association for Computing Machinery
8. Konstantinidis EI, Petsani D, Bamidis PD (2021) Teaching university students co-creation and living lab methodologies through experiential learning activities and preparing them for RRI. Health Informatics J https://doi.org/10.1177/1460458221991204

Ciência Viva—Promoting Marine Activities Around Lisbon: Self-Constructed Boats

Gonçalo Praça

Marine sports and activities for recreation, instruction, and tourism, among others, play a key role in increasing ocean literacy—the awareness of the mutual influence of ocean and human well-being. Recognising that marine leisure activities are relatively uncommon in Portugal and in Lisbon, compared with other activities and cities with similar geography, *Ciência Viva* proposed 'Kayaks to the River!', a series of workshops for building life-sized, usable kayaks, and designing activities with such boats to be part of a science festival in the river. The solution involves schools, clubs and citizens in the creation of a format for this initiative.

1 Introduction

Portugal is a coastal country famous for its mild weather and sunny beaches. The ocean plays a central role in its history, and its national mythologies and culture.

Compared to other countries and cities with similar geography, however, marine leisure activities are uncommon here. The Tejo estuary, bordering the capital Lisbon, one of the largest estuaries in Western Europe, is prepared for contemplation, not interaction. Public access to the water surface for recreational purposes is limited; current infrastructure and equipment are usually private and located in just a few locations.

G. Praça (✉)
Ciência Viva, Pavilhão Do Conhecimento, Lisbon, Portugal
e-mail: gpraca@cienciaviva.pt

A. Deserti et al. (eds.), *Co-creation for Responsible Research and Innovation*,
Springer Series in Design and Innovation 15,
https://doi.org/10.1007/978-3-030-78733-2_10

2 Ecosystem, Context and Challenge Addressed

"Giving back the river Tejo to the city" is a recurrent theme in the governance of the city, frequently picked up by researchers, the tourism industry, pundits, and policymakers. The public has asked for access to the river, for instance in proposals for marine infrastructures and services regularly submitted to municipal participatory budgets. Urban regeneration projects for parts of the city, like Parque das Nações, the neighbourhood surrounding *Ciência Viva's* headquarters has explicitly included—at least in theory—the development of recreational activities in the river.

Ciência Viva, the Portuguese agency for scientific culture, has been involved in EU and national projects to develop "ocean literacy," i.e., raising awareness of the mutual influence of the ocean and human lives. Most of these projects, often directed to young participants, rest on top-down public engagement methodologies and goals: informal education with limited dialog and interaction between the public and experts, basic consultation devices and occasional hands on activities, showing experiments with citizen science and maker activities. These initiatives seldom propose direct interaction with maritime environments.

2.1 Challenge

In Portugal, activities in the ocean or in a big river like Tejo still tend to be considered either elitist, accessible to the rich; or as dangerous, deadly and connoted with poor, uneducated people. However, the idea of nurturing a "marine culture" has permeated policy agendas at the national, city and neighbourhood level. In Lisbon, for instance, historically, the Port Authority (a publicly owned limited company) rules access to the river. New regulation is coming into force that transfers some of the ruling power to the Municipality, or even to the neighbourhood, pursuing an agenda of urban sustainability in terms of leisure, tourism, mobility, spatial planning. This agenda has the scope of increasing sports practice, raising environmental awareness and fostering civic care for public spaces.

This tension was noted in projects for "ocean literacy" in which *Ciência Viva* has been involved. Marine sports and activities for recreation, fun, instruction or tourism are crucial to increase "ocean literacy." However, to obtain any meaningful impact in engaging the public with ocean literacy, marine leisure activities must be widely and regularly practiced and be easily accessible—which does not happen in Portugal.

Members of *Ciência Viva* team wanted to address this gap, and the lab set itself a challenge that resonates with these ideas: how to devise interesting, mobilising, safe and accessible experiences in Tejo, especially in the section of the river close to Pavilion of Knowledge.

3 The Co-Creation Journey

3.1 Context Analysis

Analysis of the context rested on desk- and field research. Desk research focused on the considerable body of research and "gray" literature on recreational boating and water-based sports in Portugal and in Lisbon are, including statistics, reports, dissertations, papers, propaganda, etc. mainly from researchers in geography and urban planning; tourism; economy and innovation; cultural heritage; and sports.

Field research included interviews with key stakeholders previously identified, in particular individuals from professional networks and citizens familiar with maritime activities in the area of Lisbon, Portugal or other countries. A crucial dimension of fieldwork was the observation of the actual "design" of the river and its uses in the area of Lisbon, documenting it with photos, short videos and field notes. This included active participation in activities to address problems pertinent to the challenge.

All the material gathered was organised with basic qualitative coding techniques, identifying themes and trends, mapping stakeholders, and comparing and merging different SWOT analysis.

3.2 Problem Framing

To revise and refine the initial challenge of engaging the public with the river, the root problem of restricted active use of the river was untangled. Themes emerging in this phase revealed two major dimensions of the problem: limited physical access to water (due to inappropriate infrastructure and real or perceived costs); and a hazy yet meaningful "cultural" resistance to water-based activities.

Two main tools helped synthesising this information:

1. A SWOT analysis of leisure water activities in Portugal, in Lisbon and in the specific neighborhood, making visible dimensions of the problem that the co-lab could address meaningfully; and
2. A detailed stakeholder map with a clear idea of the interests, needs, skills and relationships between current and potential stakeholders. This helped reframe the initial challenge to make it more workable and related to specific people and groups.

The initial challenge was substantially reframed during a workshop with core stakeholders. At this stage, the challenge was "How can we show that the river in this part of the city is interesting, accessible and safe—but that it needs attention from authorities for its fruition."

Finally, the internal team further refined this challenge with the participants of an idea generation workshop. The challenge that eventually guided the idea generation was "**What interesting, mobilising, safe and accessible experiences could our co-lab create in the river in this part of the city?**"

Reframing the problem, in short, meant turning it from a general concern for promoting "ocean literacy" into something that should consider the specific needs and aspirations identified in fieldwork. The ambition was now reasonably clear: to show that the river is there, and it should be used, even if measures are needed; inviting people to literally get themselves immersed in the water; and to deploy engaging examples, instead of repeating worn-out publicity campaigns.

3.3 Envisioning Solutions

Stakeholders and internal team members imagined possible solutions from the very start of the project: it seemed natural to think of a problem by thinking of solutions, inspiring internal discussions that lead to both different perspectives on the challenge and to other ideas, one of which would later resurface during more formal ideation sessions.

In the second workshop, 13 participants discussed and wrote ideas on cards answering the question: "What interesting, mobilising, safe and accessible experiences could theco-lab create in the river in this part of the city?" The group categorised solution cards in a matrix with quadrants representing the challenge (access to sea/river; mobilisation; safety; interest). A trend started to emerge, with most ideas placed in the areas titled "interest" and "mobilisation."

The group agreed that the more promising cluster in terms of benefits was the set of solutions that involved immersive experience in the river as it is now, without complex and expensive interventions. This has been taken as an invitation to develop a solution addressing the need to show and communicate that the river is offering various possibilities already interesting and accessible. In short, to devise activities in the river capable of mobilising diverse publics, using available infrastructure and equipment, while drawing the attention of authorities for improving this equipment and infrastructure.

Another workshop with the participation of around 150 citizens (families, in particular) explored the question "Why would I want to attend an event in the river? What activities in it would move me?" to identify recurring and similar ideas and concepts most fitting to users' needs.

The solution resulting from these meetings was thus devised as an annual workshop for constructing life-sized, usable watercrafts. The boats should be exhibited in the water, in different uses, contextualised by a multidisciplinary festival devoted to the river/sea.

3.4 Developing and Prototyping

Just as the solution was emerging, the internal team came across an interesting, but barely known project, Abraçar o Vento ("Embracing the wind") [1]. The project stems from a partnership with Marquesa de Alorna,[1] a lower secondary school in Lisbon, the nautical club Boa-Esperança,[2] and GIRA,[3] a nonprofit association for the rehabilitation of adult mental disease patients [2–4]. Abraçar o Vento aims at fostering informal peer-to-peer learning to raise awareness about water sports and environmental protection, and promote social inclusion—all this around a DIY kayak workshop hosted by the school, in which students, adult patients, a carpenter and a "mentor" build complete kayaks based on an open-access template.

This encounter had profound implications for the solution. Indeed, development and prototyping phases were devoted to understanding how to generalise, expand and innovate from this learning experiment in *Ciência Viva's* own workshop-with-festival.

Discussions involving partners and stakeholders like the municipality, associations related to amateur boat-building and nautical leisure activities, teachers, and a video producer of a documentary on social innovation guided prototyping of an annual festival based on the construction of DIY kayaks built upon the experiment of the school running for the (interrupted) school year of 2019–2020. In practice, developing and prototyping included partial immersion in key moments of kayak construction with students and adult patients in a real setting; this also involved stakeholders in one workshop, and during later incursions to the school.

The team deliberately looked for simple visual tools, accessible to the internal team, stakeholders, and other staff from *Ciência Viva* to develop the solution: mind maps, storyboards, user journey maps and, in later stages of prototyping, digital mockups, and service blueprint templates. For the work on the tools and discussions of emerging results, the working group used material and virtual feedback walls, all organised around clear dimensions: like/would like/issues and doubts/suggestions, needs/requirements, goals, etc.

Developing and prototyping brought some light on aspects of the learning module, especially four main topics:

- Motivation for participation (final users and stakeholders);
- Identification of contents, material and the network needed to put the initiative in practice;
- Resources needed for the learning process (templates, tutorials, live training);
- Adaptability of the module (different versions, templates, adaptation to various situations).

Despite all restrictions due to the COVID-19 outbreak, workshops with stakeholders and colleagues offered important guidance for the service that was being

---

[1] agmarquesadealorna.wixsite.com/marquesadealorna.

[2] www.ncbe.pt/index.html.

[3] www.gira.org.pt/.

prototyped. Main instructions following from these workshops include: allow and stimulate peer-to-peer-learning, learning by doing with others; use peer-to-peer-engagement, i.e. showing, motivating, changing attitudes by example; and trying and failing—instead of the successful reproduction of existing safe models.

Initially, the solution focused on a festival that should populate the river with usable kayaks, built by teams according to a tested template. The contact with the school, and subsequent discussions with other partners, led to a much stronger emphasis on the peer-to-peer learning processes that should occur during the co-design and construction of kayaks. This, in turn, should translate into the design of contents of the festival itself as well.

3.5   The Role of Policies and Policymaker Engagement

Initial reports of the lab with policymakers—the municipality and the neighbourhood governments—piggybacked on the collaboration and personal networks between local policymakers and *Ciência Viva*. Perhaps for this reason, early engagement was straightforward; policymakers were open to meetings and expressed interest in collaborating, gave insightful information and offered to help in activities like dissemination or events in the neighbourhood.

Furthermore, it helped the challenge and, later, the developed solution, fit the agendas of different departments of the Municipality (Environment, Sports, Sea economy) of "giving back the river to the people." Local policymakers consider *Ciência Viva* a well-regarded influencer and expressed their trust in it to help to raise public interest in these activities, and to help lobby for improving public access to the river.

Once the solution became clearer, it was possible to raise the interest of a team of the municipality and national ministries involved in the organisation of a major event in Lisbon: The UN Ocean Conference that would occur within the period of the pilot. While the initiatives were cancelled due to the pandemic, the team discussed with them how to include the solution in the agenda of this event, as a pilot version of the workshop-festival. It was also considered how such an initiative could become part of a national agenda for ocean literacy.

Involving policymakers into actual co-creation turned out to be more complicated: a lack of participation in events and the support of concrete ideas for initiatives hindered their active involvement.

On the other hand, they were important to validate initial stages of the prototype: when addressing the solution in workshops or individual interviews, policymakers from the City and neighbourhood offered important suggestions to make it more realistic and implementable considering specific financial and organisational constraints that they know well.

A specific challenge related to the engagement of policymakers was ensuring a safe and comfortable space for them during the journey. In Lisbon, there are just a few actors in the fields of water leisure activities and ocean literacy; and they carry with them a history of unaddressed past and present issues. All these dimensions emerged during the journey, not without some tensions, in exchanges between policymakers and other stakeholders.

4 Experimentation: Output, Transformations, Outcomes

Ciência Viva proposes to develop an **annual festival devoted to the DIY design, adaptation and/or construction of real size kayaks** usable in rivers or similar conditions. The initiative starts with a call directed to the school community in Greater Lisbon, in particular teachers, students and staff involved with *Ciência Viva.* Participants will contribute by building collaborations for the co-construction of kayaks, and document their experiences to share them with others.

Looking at this concept as a service, it encompasses:

- An **online learning and engagement module** focused on boat design, building and co-creation skills, dissemination;
- Show and tell, "make happen" activities: **demos and workshops** for the public about DIY boat building and related skills;
- And the dissemination of **awareness and advocacy initiatives** for engagement in creative citizenship in the river.

The learning module should be used—and developed—in the school year, while the festival would be an annual event before the summer break.

An important value of the solution is embedding the ideals of co-creation deeply within the participants' experience; they will be challenged to create and develop contents for all components of the initiative—learning processes, documenting and dissemination and engagement.

Participants should work in multi-stakeholder teams, exploring diversity in gender, age and skills, recruited in their schools and their creative ecosystem, like makerspaces, local associations or even businesses. They will be invited to add as many creative "layers" as they wish, developing their kayaks in terms of design, materials, artistic dimensions, uses, and activities for the festival.

This work will be fully documented and made available on the project's site to feed the learning module itself and foster future participation in the initiative. Ultimately, participants will be encouraged to develop, complement or revise contents offered in the site (e.g., manuals, tutorials), with their ideas and creative work (including "making of," things that did not work), much in the spirit of recent open DIY innovation platforms like wikifactory.com or www.scopesdf.org.

The technical core of the solution is the online peer-to-peer learning and engagement module, planned to have five main sections:

- **Kayaks to the river!** Presenting the initiative; how to participate; steps of the creative process; submitting proposals; rules; calendar.

- **Mission** A "manifesto" for the active and creative citizenship in the river, and how it can translate into the participant's missions: design, transform, build your own kayak, and co-create the final event.
- **Resources** Set of resources to help design, building and transforming kayaks, including specific tools for (remote) creative work. Continuously updated by participants, a wiki for DIY kayak construction.
- **Galleries** Photos and videos of/by participants, about their creative journeys.
- **Help** Ongoing FAQ, fed by issues raised by participants. Contacts, including contacts for "mentors" selected from relevant stakeholders of the lab.

The online module represents a typical creative journey: participants get familiar and interested in the initiative to then form teams and define specific goals reflecting on the values stated in the initiative's manifesto, and inspired by examples offered on the site. They choose formats, materials and tools to present a summary of the idea and composition of the team. They then develop their proposals—in sketches, CAD, to scale or real-size physical prototypes, etc.—with resources (tools, tutorials, templates, etc.) available. "Mentors" selected by a pool of the lab's stakeholders are available along the process. Participants will document the development of their proposals, to feed both an ongoing wiki for DIY kayak construction and the multimedia galleries showing their creative journeys. Proposals are submitted and reviewed by lab's stakeholders and mentors, who will provide relevant feedback. Participants then work on their final models of the kayaks. Two not mutually exclusive scenarios for this work can be anticipated: (1) the models, and related activities designed by the participants will provide the contents of a weekend event in the river; or, worst-case, pandemic scenario (2) the models and related documentation will feed an online event.

4.1 Transformations Triggered

Before SISCODE, co-creation in *Ciência Viva* was an ideal that some of its staff were more or less familiar with; and selected aspects of it, rather than complete processes, were used in single tasks of several RRI projects. It is still premature to speak of permanent transformations within the organisation fed by the spirit of co-creation, and changes induced by the pandemic added a layer of uncertainty in this regard. Still, it is fair to say that *Ciência Viva* started developing more explicit, deliberate, reflexive co-creation processes during the pilot—and thanks to it.

The metaphor of the co-creation journey, and the methodologies and tools developed in the process were presented to staff members not familiar with SISCODE in informal environments to foster their spread beyond the project. These methodologies and tools were also shared and used in the following situations:

- Co-creation for Science Centers and Museums: training workshop using the metaphor of co-creation journey, and selected canvases from the toolbox;

- A class in the MSc degree in science communication at Universidade Nova de Lisboa;
- Idea generation for 2020s programme: day-long meeting(s) of *Ciência Viva's* Outreach unit;
- Co-creating engagement strategies for a Science Center with "hot topics": trial co-creation session with *Ciência Viva's* Outreach and Education units;
- Developing a programme for a national event of *Ciência Viva:* collaboration with teachers nationwide.

During the lockdown, members of *Ciência Viva* staff external to the lab joined a couple of the online workshops; for some of them, this was the first contact with co-creation methodologies. Most *Ciência Viva's* participants in the activities mentioned here expressed their wish of developing these skills with more formal training that should be provided by the organisation.

5　Lessons Learnt and Reflections

The concept of "hermeneutic circle" is particularly illuminating to describe the learning process during this experiment [5]. This refers to the idea of continually moving from smaller component parts to a larger unit, and back, in order to understand the meaning of both—the individual parts and the system as a whole. In this specific case, it becomes visible that the single components and phases of the journey have no "meaning" in themselves; the sense of the journey does not derive merely from adding up phases one after the other; rather, the importance of the journey and of the individual phases from a learning point of view can only be grasped from the complete process.

A basic implication of this idea is that the lab (and colleagues not necessarily involved in SISCODE) reached the end of the experiment much more aware of the specific skills and knowledge that should still be developed to design and carry out co-creation processes in future projects.

But the concept of the hermeneutic circle also helps have a more explicit understanding of the iterative nature of co-creation, and about the specific experiment of *Ciência Viva.* For instance, the team only understood the generative power of prototyping—i.e., how engaging with actual objects and products can accelerate new ideas and new connections between different people—close to the end of the journey; but to understand this it was necessary to have abstract discussions before. Also, it is only towards the end of the process that issues and ideas that emerged early in the journey could be taken into account.

For instance, participants in the first co-creation sessions stated along these lines: "The best way to teach someone how to swim is throwing them to the water, pardon my French, but if you want to engage people with the river that's the only way to do it"; or this: "We shouldn't waste our time with more campaigns, we have to put the public to use to show other people how this is fun"; or: "We should all go to the river, a big parade, then people outside would see us, 'Ah, that looks fun, I want to do it!'". It was only after several trial and error phases that these ideas could be fully understood; it took the whole "circle" to make justice to the aspirations they reflected.

References

1. Abraçar o Vento. bit.ly/2CNEZFM. Last accessed 02 Oct 2020
2. GIRA. www.gira.org.pt/. Last accessed 02 Oct 2020
3. Marquesa de Alorna School. agmarquesadealorna.wixsite.com/marquesadealorna. Last accessed 02 Oct 2020
4. Nautical club Boa-Esperança. www.ncbe.pt/index.html. Last accessed 02 Oct 2020
5. University of Leiden. The hermeneutic circle. https://www.youtube.com/watch?v=zIEzc__BBxs. Last accessed 29 Mar 2021

Cube Design Museum—Empathic Co-design for Societal Impact

Anja Köppchen

Cube design museum addresses current and future challenges within the broader context of an ageing and shrinking society, to improve the quality of life of people of all ages. This chapter presents the development of a tool, to stimulate and facilitate new, participatory ways of policymaking, to drive citizen engagement and bottom-up social innovation: the Co-Design Canvas. It has been co-designed and tested within the context of the village of Ransdaal in the Netherlands.

1 Introduction

Located in Kerkrade, a small town in the south-eastern corner of the Netherlands, next to the German border and about 15 km from Belgium, *Cube design museum*[1] has been the first Dutch museum to be entirely dedicated to design. From 2015–2020, the museum was one of three institutions, including Columbus earth center and Continium discovery center, governed by the Museumplein Limburg Foundation, which is partly funded by the province of Limburg (regional government). Museumplein Limburg aims to empower citizens, by contributing to their social self-confidence, economic self-reliance, and cultural awareness. It addresses questions

---

[1] Since 2021, Cube design museum is no longer operational, due to restructuring as a consequence of the Covid-19 crisis. Museumplein Limburg has combined its formerly three institutions into a new concept: Discovery Museum (www.discoverymuseum.nl).

The author is highly indebted to prof. Wina Smeenk (Inholland University of Applied Sciences), for her indispensable role in developing the Co-Design Canvas and thereby also in shaping the outcomes and learnings of Cube's co-design journey.

A. Köppchen (✉)
Discovery Museum, Kerkrade, Netherlands
e-mail: a.koppchen@discoverymuseum.nl

© The Author(s) 2022

A. Deserti et al. (eds.), *Co-creation for Responsible Research and Innovation*,
Springer Series in Design and Innovation 15,
https://doi.org/10.1007/978-3-030-78733-2_11

and challenges related to the earth, sustainability, science, technology, and design in the context of society, industry and education. More specifically, *Cube* focused on design for human needs and ambitions; i.e. design with societal impact.

The development of *Cube* coincided with a gradually growing awareness among the (international) museum community that museums need to constantly rethink their role and value for society, which requires more participatory approaches to actively engage the public [1, 7]. *Cube design museum* did not only exhibit artifacts of design in the context of several social and environmental developments and challenges, but focused particularly on the process of design and its underlying needs and ambitions for societal change. A crucial part of the museum space was therefore dedicated to the design labs, where students and designers co-created with museum visitors and other stakeholders to tackle current and future societal challenges, based on design thinking and human-centred design. Evoking dialogue and debate with and among museum visitors was an important part of *Cube's* focus and practice.

The aim of SISCODE to experiment with a design-driven approach to co-creation in the fields of RRI and policymaking in different contexts throughout Europe provided an opportunity for *Cube* and Museumplein Limburg to both test and further enhance its capacity to engage multiple stakeholders in the process of design for societal impact. The project thus also served as a pilot to further explore the museum's role to empower citizens in the region to tackle current and future challenges.

In the context of the region's social challenges, *Cube* started this project with the aim to improve the quality of life of people living and growing up in an ageing society. Together with the nearby municipality of Voerendaal and citizens of one of its villages Ransdaal, the project gradually became more focused towards citizen participation and public engagement as being preconditions for a future proof society and quality of life for all citizens. In collaboration with municipal policymakers and highly engaged citizens, *Cube* re-framed the aim to design a tool that can stimulate and facilitate new, participatory ways of policymaking, in order to drive citizen engagement and bottom-up initiatives. The project resulted in the development of the Co-Design Canvas: a tool for openly and transparently initiating, planning, conducting and assessing collaborations around societal challenges with multiple stakeholders. In short: an empathic co-design tool with societal impact.

2   Ecosystem, Context and Challenge Addressed

Cube's co-design journey needs to be understood in the context of the Netherlands' increasing political focus on citizen participation and the Limburg region's social challenges related to an ageing and shrinking population. The South Limburg region is a former coal mining area and constitutes the south-eastern periphery of the Netherlands. Since the shutdown of the mining industry in the 1960s and 1970s, Limburg has been going through several economic transitions, including the development of the chemical industry, smart services and leisure industries. Next to the region's economic development, Limburg is facing considerable demographic challenges due to a shrinking and ageing population.

Population ageing provides a variety of socio-economic policy challenges for EU, national, regional and local governments alike [3, 5, 11]. When the population is not only ageing but also shrinking, as is the case in South Limburg, the pressure on public services becomes even more apparent and social developments like increasing feelings (or fear) of loneliness add to the challenges' complexity.

In the last decades, the Netherlands is aiming to make a transition from a welfare state to a participation society, in which citizens are expected to take more responsibility for their own lives and surroundings [12]. Increasing focus on citizen involvement and public engagement in both national and local policy programmes is the result of a combination of austerity measures and a gradually changing perspective on how a healthy and sustainable society should function [2]. The role of the government and its relation to citizens is thus changing and new ways of interaction and collaboration are needed.

The small town of Voerendaal (approx. 12,500 inhabitants), which consists of five smaller villages, presents an exemplary case of the more widespread regional challenges as described above. The municipality's increasing need and desire to unfold more participatory ways of policymaking with the aim to improve its citizens' quality of life, in addition to their willingness to experiment and a highly engaged group of citizens in the village of Ransdaal (approx. 900 inhabitants), provided a good starting point for *Cube's* co-design journey.

In collaboration with Voerendaal policymakers from the social domain and a group of Ransdaal citizens including a citizens cooperative, *Cube's* initial challenge became more and more focused and contextualised. From the start, policymakers and citizens shared the ambition to create and maintain a liveable and future-proof village. While a small group of Ransdaal citizens is highly engaged and employs many bottom-up initiatives, there is also the ambition to increase engagement and support among the entire community. There are always too many ideas and not enough people and resources. At the same time, the municipality is looking for ways to give its citizens more space to take matters into their own hands. In sum, policymakers and citizens felt the need to improve their collaboration and coordination of initiatives. The more concrete and re-framed aim of this co-design project became, therefore, to design a tool that can stimulate and facilitate new, participatory ways of policymaking, to drive citizen engagement and bottom-up initiatives.

3 The Co-creation Journey

Co-design processes are inherently iterative. For complex societal challenges, there is no one right solution available, which asks for an open-ended, non-linear approach. The four phases that have been defined in the SISCODE project of *context analysis, problem reframing, envisioning solutions,* and *prototype development* have served as guiding principles for planning and reflection in and on *Cube's* co-design journey.

But the boundaries between these phases are blurred and most of the co-design practices focus on different phases simultaneously and involve a continuous back and forth between exploring, understanding, envisioning and creating. Therefore, instead of describing the process in a linear way as four subsequent phases,[2] this section will highlight some key aspects and challenges that defined the evolution of *Cube's* co-design journey as an iterative learning experience.

3.1 Framing and Reframing

Starting from the broad context of quality of life in an ageing society, *Cube's* co-design journey involved a long phase of exploring different directions, contexts and (geographical) scopes. Different types of potential stakeholders were involved, including museum visitors, students, designers, researchers, and local and regional policymakers. This led to a large collection of needs, ambitions, questions and ideas, varying from highly personal or technical ideas, such as a robot play buddy for lonely children among an ageing population, to more conceptual ideas for a participatory community such as a future citizen lab. Especially the first half of the journey has been a process of constantly diverging and converging, of zooming in and zooming out.

To facilitate this process with different groups of stakeholders, *Cube* regularly used the tool of Frameboards [9]. This canvas has become part of a well-established method at the *Cube* design labs to turn the process of framing into a conscious practice. The Frameboard Canvas is used to capture and visualise both the challenge and possible solution spaces and ideas for specific target groups, which then serves as a boundary object [10] to reflect on the ideas with other stakeholders. In this way, frameboards facilitate the iterative and exploratory nature of the process in which ideation and re-framing is part of the same process that Stompff calls 'learning by creating' [9]. Every workshop, conversation, prototype, or test generated new ideas that brought the team closer to a solution, while it also increased the team's understanding of the challenge and its underlying factors. One of the most significant reframing processes in *Cube's* journey took place in close collaboration with the municipality of Voerendaal and the citizens of Ransdaal, which led to a shift from ageing to the question of citizen participation as a way to support quality of life in a more future oriented context. However, even with this more concrete context defined, it took many rounds of reframing, envisioning, and reflection, before the first version of the final prototype took shape.

---

[2] For a more comprehensive description of Cube's activities and challenges in the four co-design phases, see chapter 4.8 of the SISCODE deliverable 3.4 [6].

3.2 Tools and Sites for Co-Creation

In a co-design process, various stakeholders collaborate and co-create to tackle societal challenges through participatory and creative methods. The SISCODE toolbox provides a comprehensive collection of existing (design) tools to support this process. In addition to the frameboards as discussed above, *Cube* has experimented with many tools and methods both from the SISCODE toolbox and beyond [13], with varying results. *Cube* learned that the efficacy of such tools largely depends on the situation and the preference and knowledge of participants and facilitators. Whichever tools were used, their main role has been to provide a shared language and understanding among the participants, to make sense of data, and to evoke new perspectives and collective creativity. Working with different tools in several workshops led to many tangible outcomes including mood boards, mind maps, customer journeys and rapid prototypes. Making ideas tangible and visual has been extremely important to keep stakeholders engaged, helping them to better grasp the potential value of an intended solution.

Along with the tools, the settings in which *Cube* organised co-design and co-creation activities affected the process and outcomes, which points to the role of space and place in human interactions. For *Cube's* journey, three types of sites for co-creation were selected or established: the creative lab spaces of *Cube* design museum, locations within the context of the challenge (i.e. Voerendaal and Ransdaal), and virtual spaces through online activities. Each site comes with specific opportunities and limitations.

The *Cube* design labs provided a creative, inspirational and flexible space that enables people to get out of their daily routines and thus see things in a different light. In addition to inviting stakeholders to the lab for a workshop or co-design session, *Cube* also used the space to organise informal and spontaneous sessions with museum visitors who were not directly involved in the challenge. This provided the team with new insights and reflections from a broader perspective. While the lab can inspire and encourage people to get out of their comfort zones and bring in new perspectives, it can also be a threshold for some to participate, precisely because it is distant from the real context. *Cube* organised several sessions in the local community centre of Ransdaal, which provided a familiar and safe space for especially those citizens who might not feel comfortable to enter into a design process, and where the barrier to participate is literally smaller. To encourage the creative process, tools and methods were brought into the village, which created very similar opportunities as the labs in Kerkrade. The third type of location has been created out of necessity, as a consequence of the meeting limitations due to the COVID-19 pandemic since March 2020. There are obvious advantages, because there is no need for physical spaces and travelling, and it has made recording and storing of outcomes much easier. However, *Cube* also encountered significant challenges, especially in terms of limited human interaction and inclusivity. Still, even though online conversations cannot replace real-life interactions, experimenting extensively with different online tools increased *Cube's* knowledge and expertise, and provided a valuable addition to its already familiar collaboration tools and ways of working.

3.3 Stakeholder Engagement: Learning About Power, Trust and Empathy

As has already been stressed, co-design is about engaging multiple stakeholders in a collaborative endeavour to achieve positive change. The most important stakeholders in *Cube's* journey to achieve new, participatory ways of policymaking and to drive citizen engagement and bottom-up initiatives, were municipal policymakers and citizens. The groups of stakeholders participating in the co-design sessions organised by *Cube* varied in size and composition. Many participants were not involved throughout the whole process. Eventually, only a small number of highly dedicated stakeholders were closely involved in developing and testing the final prototype. This group consisted of three policymakers from the department of social development at the municipality of Voerendaal (one alderman and two civil servants) and five highly motivated citizens of the village of Ransdaal, including members of the citizens cooperative 'Ransdaal voor Elkaar'.

This evolution of participating stakeholders presents an important learning outcome. Although the workshops were considered successful in terms of providing new insights based on open and constructive dialogue, they also caused frustration and scepticism among some citizens and policymakers. It turned out challenging for people to get into the flow of design thinking, embracing an open-ended process, and not to expect immediate and concrete results. *Cube* thus learned about the need to manage expectations, to prevent drop-outs throughout the process.

Another challenge in terms of stakeholder engagement relates to questions of power and trust. Unequal power relations were sensed frequently during workshops. But it was only in the later phases of the journey when the prototype of the Co-Design Canvas was being tested, that these power relations were openly and explicitly addressed. This resulted in an increased awareness among stakeholders about their different roles and perceptions, and about how stakeholders' different languages can lead to misconceptions and a lack of trust and understanding.

Cube involved empathic co-design expert Wina Smeenk [8] in the last phase of the journey to address these challenges, to support the team by organising and facilitating co-design sessions, and by designing a testable prototype. Citizens and policymakers were in need for more guidance in co-designing new ways of working and collaborating. In particular the group of Ransdaal citizens indicated the need of a clear co-design process for their citizen initiatives and the need to make the process more tangible for testing. Initiated by Wina Smeenk and inspired by the *Design Choices Framework* of Lee et al. [4], the Co-Design Canvas was being developed through several rounds of (online) testing between March and November 2020.

4 Experimentation: Output, Transformations, Outcomes

The Co-Design Canvas is a tool that supports the facilitation of an open, transparent dialogue about all stakeholders' experiences and interests, the alignment of expectations and goals, the creation of insights and understanding, and the exchange of knowledge, power relations and shared responsibilities in planning, conducting and assessing a co-design process. Throughout its journey, *Cube* learned that problems in collaborative processes often arise from tensions between the people and organisations involved, for instance due to power imbalance or (social) contingencies that evolve, were not foreseen nor discussed beforehand. The canvas can clarify these issues and relationships, and offer those involved stakeholders a common language and method to reflect on and in the process. Co-design processes require dialogue, transparency, and empathy. The Co-Design Canvas can help facilitate these processes and create insight into why processes succeed or fail (Fig. 1).

The design of the canvas is aiming at a comprehensive, yet flexible and easy to use tool, that can be adopted to different contexts, needs, and phases of the process. It identifies eight interdependent variables that influence the process: the context, the purpose of change, the stakeholders, the results, the impact, and the co-design focus, setting, and activities. The canvas integrates these variables into process cards, which can be discussed separately, without a fixed order. After all, a co-design project is an iterative and joint learning process. When put together, the cards create one canvas to see the bigger picture and address the relations between the variables. The front of the cards contain guiding questions to stimulate the discussion, providing room to write, draw, or put sticky notes. On the back there is more information about each card's purpose, as well as some tips & tricks and additional tools to get stakeholders started. These include tools from the SISCODE toolbox and other design thinking and social innovation methods. Building on the iterative and open-ended nature of a co-design process, the canvas is a dynamic tool that can and should be used multiple times

Fig. 1 The co-design canvas (left) and a schematic representation of the canvas cards (right)

during different phases and whose content is constantly changing. The Co-Design Canvas is a tool for initiating, planning, conducting and assessing collaborations around societal challenges with multiple stakeholders openly and transparently.

5   Lessons Learnt and Reflections

One of the underlying assumptions of the SISCODE project and of *Cube's* pilot, is that co-design approaches can support an effective interaction between policymakers, citizens and other stakeholders. Drawing on the museum's experience with design thinking and co-creation, this project provided a valuable opportunity for *Cube* to further explore and develop its potential role in these kinds of multi-stakeholder collaborations. Several enthusiastic reactions from different stakeholders and policy and research institutions who have tried and tested different versions of the canvas, have encouraged the organisation to continue developing its participatory approach with artists, designers, researchers, policymakers, and last but not least citizens.

The Co-Design Canvas was produced in physical form under Creative Commons licence in February 2021. In addition to the eight cards, it consists of a booklet that contains practical guidance and illustrated instructions to support the actual use of the canvas by different stakeholders. However, even though considerable time and effort has gone into testing and revising this prototype to make it as practical and intuitive as possible, the tool itself doesn't make an impact. It can only support social change, which ultimately requires changing mindsets and practice.

Both policymakers and citizens have expressed their motivations to use the Co-Design Canvas in future citizen initiatives and participation strategies. But there has been no clear agreement on how to further develop and implement it in a collaborative manner. It seems that equal collaboration between citizens and policymakers is not yet an established routine, which confirms one of *Cube's* experiences that changing relations and expectations, as well as creating trust and understanding takes time and a certain openness to change and reframe.

In order to structurally implement more participatory ways of policymaking furthermore requires different ways of working across the municipality, including other departments like spatial planning. This involves some political decision making as well. Moreover, the municipality's civil servants have indicated that they might need more support or training on how to facilitate working with the canvas. They have set up a preliminary implementation plan, which includes a workshop facilitated by *Cube*, to introduce the tool and methodology to a more diverse group of policymakers within the municipality. They will then work with the canvas in different projects for a specified period of time, after which the method and experiences will be evaluated.

Sustainable implementation thus takes more time and practice. And with time and practice, the Co-Design Canvas might (or should?) change as well, which is part of an iterative learning process. After all, a tool is just a tool. The best tools, methods or procedures are of no use if they don't fit the mindset and attitude of the participating stakeholders or if there is a lack of respect, equality, and empathy.

References

1. Bunnik C (2014) Musea voor Mensen. Museumvereniging, Amsterdam, Amsterdam
2. De Haan E, Meier S, Haartsen T, Strijker D (2018) Defining 'success' of local citizens initiatives in maintaining public services in rural areas: a professional's perspective. Sociologia Ruralis 58:312–330
3. Kotzeva M et al (2015) People in the EU: who are we and how do we live? Publications Office of the European Union, Luxembourg
4. Lee J-J et al (2018) Design choices framework for co-creation projects. Int J Des 12(2):15–31
5. Meuwissen J, Severijns B, Gardeniers J (2017) Begeleidende notitie bij de resultaten van Progneff. Etil Research Group, Maastricht
6. Real M et al (2020) SISCODE deliverable 3.4: experimentation report—Lab's journeys as case-studies
7. Simon N (2010) The participatory Museum. Museum 2.0
8. Smeenk W (2019) Navigating empathy: empathic formation in co-design. Doctoral Dissertation, Eindhoven University of Technology
9. Stompff G (2018) Design thinking: radicaal veranderen in kleine stappen. Boom uitgevers, Amsterdam, Amsterdam
10. Stompff G (2020) De Kracht van Verbeelden: design thinking in teams [inaugural speech, 27 Nov 2020]. Inholland University of Applied Sciences
11. Te Riele S et al (2019) PBL/CBS Regionale bevolkings-en huishoudensprognose 2019–2050. Statistics Netherlands, The Hague
12. Van Houwelingen P, Boele A, Dekker P (2014) Burgermacht op eigen kracht? Een brede verkenning van ontwikkelingen in burgerparticipatie. Netherlands Institute for Social Research (SCP), The Hague
13. Willenborg A, Smeenk W (2017) Shake it! Een design thinking-spel voor innovatie en transformatie. Boom Uitgevers, Amsterdam

Science Gallery Dublin—Open Mind: Improving Mental Health of Young People

Grace D'Arcy and Ilaria Mariani

To face the challenge of improving mental health and well-being with young people, *Science Gallery Dublin* initiates a high-school programme for mentorship among students. Involving academics, NGO's, psychologists, parents, teachers, college and high-school students, 'Open Mind' intends to use hobbies and individual attitudes for favouring empowerment and the overall atmosphere of the school, also leading to a long-term increased well-being and fewer mental health issues. This chapter describes how this programme empowers the young people to understand the importance of hobbies for their mental health, while using co-creation techniques for them to be innovative in facilitating the clubs.

1 Introduction

1.1 The Organisation

Science Gallery Dublin (SGD) is a space for public engagement, part of Trinity College Dublin and of a worldwide network of Science Galleries, a network of leading universities devoted to ignite creativity and discovery at the crossroad of science and art. To reach this aim, *SGD* organises multidisciplinary and engaging exhibitions between the fields art and science dealing with relevant issues for young adults. For their realisation, artists, makers and researchers collaborate in the development of

G. D'Arcy (✉)
Science Gallery Dublin, Dublin, Ireland
e-mail: grace.darcy@dublin.sciencegallery.com

I. Mariani
Department of Design, Politecnico Di Milano, Milan, Italy
e-mail: ilaria1.mariani@polimi.it

© The Author(s) 2022

A. Deserti et al. (eds.), *Co-creation for Responsible Research and Innovation*,
Springer Series in Design and Innovation 15,
https://doi.org/10.1007/978-3-030-78733-2_12

these exhibitions engaging 15–25 year olds, thus creating a space of learning, discussion and imagination with the aim to develop capacities such as critical thinking, cooperation, creativity and communication skills. *SGD* frequently applies participatory methodologies to the development of its exhibitions and programmes constantly seeking to improve engagement and co-creation practices in a long-term process.

1.2   The Co-Creation Journey

Perceiving co-creation as a means for collaboration it is applied to involve, engage and learn from and together with stakeholders. As such, co-creation is a critically important approach in tackling issues. Specifically, it enabled *SGD* to reach out and connect with young people to jointly develop a solution for a specific issue relevant for them during SISCODE—young people and their mental health.

Within the frame of 'mental health and management of well-being' a group of 31 young people, teachers, parents and professionals in the field of mental health has been set up initiated through an open call to be involved throughout the project. The experimentation engaged a team of *SGD* members, and three groups of young people aged from 15–23, as well as a variety of professionals from the field of mental health and well-being. The activities started introducing the overall approach of SISCODE, its tools and methodologies to the group. For the purpose a set of Design Thinking activities and workshops were organised, allowing participants to get aligned before starting to redefine the problem and generate ideas collaboratively. Among the variety of ideas developed in the early phases, education and school was a recurring core element when speaking about well-being management of young people since school represents one of the main aspects of their life and at the same time is often a cause or driver of stress and worries. This became the issue at stake, to tackle through a co-creation approach that largely encourages bottom-up solutions.

Over the course of 18 months the group ideated, developed, prototyped, and tested a concept for an educational model for well-being management and understanding of mental health issues in second-level schools. The scope of this module is to transfer the importance of mental health to students, while connecting it to the importance of their hobbies and interests. All contents have been collaboratively developed with students and experts ranging from interactive activities to the choice of topics to be addressed in the learning module.

As part of the prototyping activities, the educational model has been iteratively tested as a pilot in four Irish schools to be then refined and improved for future application. Apart from the module, the project also led to a different application of co-creation practices and a general shift of approach in *SGD*.

2 Ecosystem, Context and Challenge Addressed

2.1 External Context and Ecosystem

During SISCODE, *SGD* experimented with co-creation to tackle the topic of mental health and its issues, establishing a direct link between the empowerment of people and improved mental health. The issue of mental health and well-being has been chosen as one of the most pressing issues in Ireland in recent times ranking third out of 36 European countries investigated [4]. The Irish government published a vision towards significant improvements in physical and mental health that considers the needs and responsibilities of citizens leading to mental health being valued and supported across all societal levels [2].

The specific focus on young people can be traced back both to the main target audience of *SGD*, 15–25 year olds, and to studies tracing mental health difficulties back to late teen- and adolescent age [3]. Mental health can also be associated with a lack of positive factors and traits such as self-esteem, absence of optimism and positive coping mechanisms, together with a general lack of consideration of the direct involvement of affected individuals and groups. Empowerment as one of the core goals of the WHO's envisioning of the development of health promotion has been stated as "People should be empowered to promote their own health, interact effectively with health services and be active partners in managing disease" [7]. Within this frame, the Irish government is addressing the issue of mental health management in young people with a strategy set out to give children and young adults a voice in co-developing policies and services that affect their well-being [1].

2.2 Organisational Background

Science Gallery Dublin is part of Ireland's internationally top-ranked university Trinity College Dublin. This inherently provides a rich variety of contacts and communication channels to reach out to researchers and professionals in combination with the relationships *SGD* established during activities and exhibitions with their target of 15–25 year olds prior to the initiation of the project. Furthermore, also the topic of mental health has already been addressed by *SGD* in the past leading to a pool of contacts, relationships and experiences to be exploited during the co-creation journey.

Apart from the multidisciplinary team within the organisation which includes scientists, artists and designers, all the *SGD* exhibitions tend to gather and to various extents engage a wide variety of external stakeholders. Engineers, designers, artists and scientists relevant to the particular topic of the exhibition are involved aiming at the constant expansion and enrichment of their network and leading to the establishment of public engagement practices together with capacities for the coordination of highly complex projects. In light of that, *SGD* has already experimented and applied co-creation, even though it lacked structure and formalisation in its implementation It has manifested mainly in the collaboration with the Leonardo group, a part of the advisory board composed by young people from across Ireland with the scope of informing the activities and directions of *SGD* through constant exchange, collaboration on initiatives and the integration of their own events in the context of the Science Gallery.

2.3   Challenge

The broad challenge of 'mental health and well-being' was chosen as one of the core themes of interest for the Science Gallery, as well as a pressing societal issue across Ireland. It has then narrowed down by conducting an extensive desk research in combination with interviews and focus groups involving stakeholders and users with various backgrounds and interests on the topic. It became evident that it is in need of being further addressed in the context of schools. As a consequence, the refined challenge around 'Co-creating mental health resources with young people to use in a school setting' has been addressed taking two different main aspects into consideration. On one hand, the challenge of supporting the students directly in developing an understanding of mental health and feeding capacities for managing their own well-being was tackled while on the other hand the policy background was addressed ideating new strategies for the inclusion of young people in the co-design of resources and policies.

3   The Co-creation Journey

The co-creation journey resulted in two main developments: an educational module was created and experimented in four Irish schools as a tangible resource of well-being management; triggered and sustained by the SISCODE methodology, the process ignited changes within *SGD* as an organisation. The evolution of both aspects throughout the four phases is described in the following.

3.1   Analysis of the Context

The initial investigation consisted in a literature review and additional desk research on the current policy landscape in Ireland. This was followed by field research involving stakeholders in interviews and focus groups, while more than sixty young people as end users have been engaged directly in hands-on workshops. The results were a clear definition of the current situation, its specific challenges, and its context in the shape of representation of data and qualitative insights, together with proto-personas of the relevant stakeholders and users identified. The elaboration of the results were then presented and discussed with those who partook in the activities. The close collaboration with the involved groups throughout the research and the presentation of results led to the establishment of relationships since the early phases, raising interest in the initiative and the overall topic.

3.2 Reframing of the Problem

The challenges have been narrowed down and reframed conducting a series of structured workshops with stakeholders and users where design thinking tools and methodologies as personas or priority mapping were applied. The participants were split in groups to foster open discussions and constructive exchange of views leading to collectively identify the specific problem to be addressed as the focus on education on the topic of mental health and well-being within the formal setting of schools. In relation to the age of the target group, one particular year in the Irish educational system has been identified as a transition year particularly suitable for the activity, being situated between two cycles of education. Moreover the focus has been identified as the improvement and fostering of self-directed and independent learning [5].

3.3 Envisioning of Alternatives

The workshops generated a plethora of different ideas among a group of users and stakeholders. Then the single ideas have then been clustered and presented to experts to be collaboratively evaluated with a SWOT analysis. The activity led to grouping and combining ideas, resulting in the final concept of developing an extracurricular mental health programme to be implemented in schools in the shape of clubs promoting hobbies to foster well-being.

3.4 Development and Prototyping

The final concept is 'OPEN MIND', a 9-week educational module developed for teachers to be implemented in schools for supporting young people in understanding and improving their well-being management through personal interests and hobbies. The entire programme revolves around four key topics: (i) empathy and inclusion skills, (ii) mental health literacy, (iii) well-being management tools, and (iv) teamwork and co-creation skills. Central is the activity of co-creating hobby clubs in schools where older students act as mentors of younger people to empower them in managing their well-being and encourage their interests and personal relations. The solution was developed focusing on one hand on the development of the content transmitted in-class through videos, on the other hand designing a roadmap for the overall prototyping of a 9-week programme of learning activities, hands-on lessons and reflective discussions carried out in four selected schools. Having identified creativity and consistency in engagement as two fundamental drivers for the improvement of mental health, students were asked to keep a diary in addition to the activities carried out in school both to provide an additional reflective tool to the students and monitor the activity itself.

In terms of monitoring and assessment, focus groups and feedback sessions were organised through the course and after the conclusion of both iterations of the programme to capture feedback and insights on the overall experience as well as on its specific elements and activities. The analysis of the results gathered was utilised to improve the programme in the following phases of the prototyping.

Between the two loops of prototyping conducted, the barriers for implementation, like the additional burden of work for teachers or the long-term sustainability in terms of training emerged. The barriers spotted have been thoroughly discussed with stakeholders leading to a transformation of the activity towards a mainly extracurricular one with few specific in-class sessions. The content of the sessions itself has been refined based on the feedback of the students, who were further involved in co-developing more engaging and appealing contents, able to better respond to their needs, expectations, and desires.

3.5 The Role of Policies and Policymaker Engagement

Policymakers have been engaged and involved throughout the entire journey, from more general, exploratory interviews in the early stages to concrete engagement of specific figures with the advanced prototype, carrying out consultation meetings and discussing concrete plans to implement OPEN MIND nationwide in schools. The positive feedback and wide interest from the policymakers' side has been reinforced by the COVID-19 pandemic that brought mental health issues and well-being management back into the focus of the government. As a result, the OPEN MIND programme has been transformed into an online resource to be distributed to a large network of schools connected to *SGD*.

4 Experimentation: Output, Transformations, Outcomes

OPEN MIND is a programme that supports students with tools and methods for developing their personal interests and hobbies. Beyond the specific aim of improving mental health and well-being management, it encourages the culture of positive well-being, resilience, student participation in decision making. Resulting in activities of co-creation of the school environment, young people played a key role in developing an innovative solution prototyped for their own context and well-being. Acknowledging the complexity of maintaining and supporting the programme and its tasks through time, specific efforts have been made to make the programme sustainable and able to operate in the long run without the direct and constant inclusion of the *SGD* team. To provide guidance and support, a guide, training materials, and specific tools have been developed. The aim is making teachers able to implement the programme independently. Such training resources will be available on the official portal of the Department of Education. In parallel it has already started the development of an exploitation strategy.

In terms of transformations triggered and outcomes, the pilot was beneficial for the *SGD* team in different ways. Firstly, it provided an occasion to experiment in-field a different approach, that of co-creation and its practices. The overall process, in conjunction with the specific topic addressed brought new knowledge and expertise concerning the direct engagement and involvement of youth voices. The impact was significant, ranging from the reinforcement of existing skills to the introduction of new ones. Indeed, the overall experimentation largely benefitted from relying on the SISCODE methods and tools.

Secondly, the knowledge and know-how gained quickly became the object of an important process of embedding this knowledge into the organisation to be applied beyond the project in other initiatives (scaling out) regarding transdisciplinary education and multi-stakeholder engagement. Applied in-presence, but also adapted for online use, due to the COVID-19 emergency which imposed a switch to in-distance activities, especially the toolkit emerged as a valuable resource for multi-stakeholder engagement. Going beyond its application within the domain of SISCODE, the toolkit has been central to supporting Open Science Hub, a Horizon 2020 project aimed at engaging schools and local stakeholders in research and innovation, the project brings science, technology, engineering, art and mathematics (STEAM) education to the communities for sustainable development. Aimed at inspiring, empowering and engaging citizens in STEAM learning and research opportunities, the project is grounded in collaborating with the local community and other stakeholders. During the COVID-19 pandemic the *SGD* team adapted the SISCODE toolkit for online use to support Open Science Hub partners in structuring their co-creation journeys with their local communities. Further online adaptations of the toolkit also occurred in the Horizon 2020 project Fostering Integration and Transformation for FOOD 2030 (FIT4FOOD 2030) that points at creating sustainable food network systems.

Finally, the SISCODE methodology and the toolkit contributed to building co-creation practices within the network of Science Galleries over time. As a matter of fact, apart from being scaled-out to other projects within the *SGD* institution, the toolkit has also been the object of a significant scaling up, being disseminated and used across the Science Gallery Network worldwide. Additionally, *Science Gallery Dublin* ran online training sessions on 'Creating Co-creation Sessions' for staff and youth advisors across the Network.

In general, the expertise gained during the SISCODE project strongly positions *SGD* nationally as a facilitator of multi-stakeholder engagement.

5 Lessons Learnt and Reflections

The experience conducted led *SGD* to reflect on the outcomes of the project regarding its ability to tackle a youth-centred issue from various points of view. Stressing the capacity building inside the organisation, the project triggered pivotal reflections concerning the mediation among stakeholders. An important lesson learnt regards facilitating balancing voices within a group and encouraging relationships to obtain conversations and discussions where all stakeholders and users meet on eye-level. Another attention point is related to the role of the mediator, as gatekeeper and facilitator for the co-creation process not only among single stakeholders, but with other organisations, like schools in this case. On the side of policies the confrontation with formal educational institutes has confirmed their lack of flexibility and agility as a potential barrier to the introduction and implementation of co-creation practices highlighting the potential of informal organisations related to education like museums or cultural organisations [6].

References

1. Department of Children and Youth Affairs (2015) National strategy on children and young people's participation in decision-making, 2015–2020
2. Department of Health (2013) A framework for improved health and wellbeing 2013–2025
3. Dooley BA, Fitzgerald A (2012) My world survey: National study of youth mental health in Ireland. Headstrong and UCD School of Psychology
4. Organisation for Economic Co-operation and Development, & European Union (2016) Health at a glance: state of health in the EU cycle. Europe 2016. OECD Publishing
5. Perkins R, Cosgrove J, Moran G, Shiel G (2012) PISA 2009: results for Ireland and changes since 2000. Educational Research Centre, Dublin
6. Sunderland Bowe JA (2016) The Creative Museum–analysis of selected best practices from Europe. Heritec Education Consulting
7. World Health Organisation (2010) User empowerment in mental health: a statement by the WHO Regional Office for Europe-empowerment is not a destination, but a journey

TRACES—In 2030, Artificial Intelligences Will Visit Museums?

Matteo Merzagora, Aude Ghilbert, and Axel Meunier

Within the SISCODE project, the science and society association *TRACES*, based in Paris, addresses the issue of making algorithms and artificial intelligence intelligible to their users. The project intends to raise awareness of algorithmic decision making in the citizen's daily life through co-creation activities involving research, education, civic right organisations and policymaking. Within general cultural activities in an art–science, provocative approach, the issue has been addressed through an inversion of perspective, by analysing people's relationship with AI when considering them as the target group of *TRACES'* cultural productions. By embedding AI as public of theatre plays and other cultural activities, *TRACES* develops a critical approach to increase the public awareness of the impact of algorithmic decision making in society, and support policymakers acting within this specific socio-technical controversy, clearly bound to remain a core issue in the years to come.

1 Algorithmic Decision Making for Cultural Activities

TRACES is a not for profit association acting at the crossroad between participatory science engagement and social inclusion. *TRACES* runs the activities of Espace des Sciences Pierre-Gilles de Gennes, the science-culture venue of ESPCI Paris and PSL Research University, a leading French research university covering a wide academic

M. Merzagora (✉) · A. Ghilbert
TRACES, Paris, France

A. Ghilbert
e-mail: aude.ghilbert@groupe-traces.fr

A. Meunier
The Center for Internet and Society (CIS), CNRS, Paris, France
e-mail: axel.meunier@cnrs.fr

A. Deserti et al. (eds.), *Co-creation for Responsible Research and Innovation*,
Springer Series in Design and Innovation 15,
https://doi.org/10.1007/978-3-030-78733-2_13

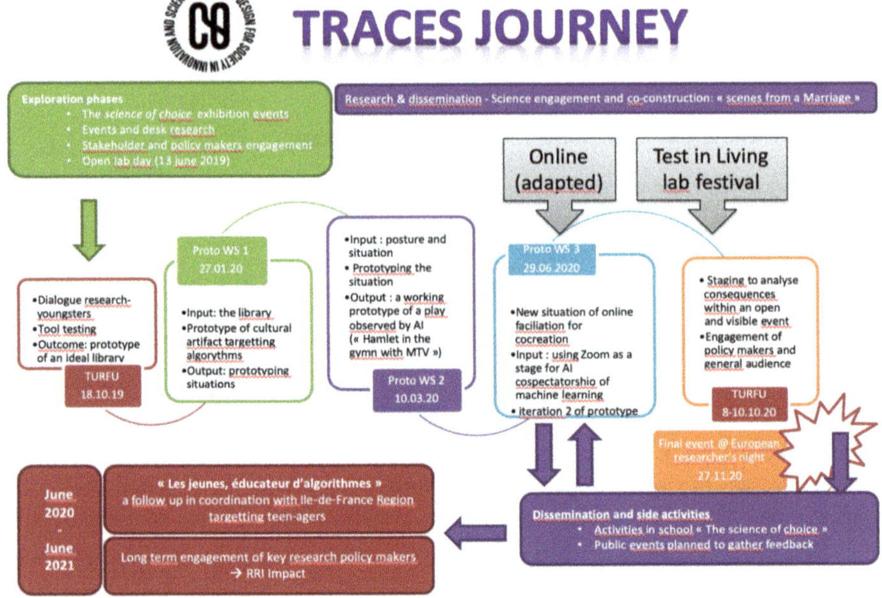

Fig. 1 TRACES' co-creation journey

field, well-connected to national research bodies and with a strong innovation-oriented research policy. *TRACES* aims to create Living Lab spaces in which to reflect, experiment and innovate in the fields of science in society, science education and public communication of science.

TRACES' journey addresses the issue of the "right to be informed" in automated decision processes using artificial intelligence in everyday life. How can the presence of AI-based supports that assist the professional or everyday life decisions become noticeable and readable for end users/citizens, so they can make informed choices in crucial aspects of their lives? As a science engagement organisation, *TRACES* identified a real need of including discussions on the topic in contexts and situations easily accessible by general audiences, such as in educational or cultural activities, and of influencing policymakers to treat the topic in a more original and empowering way.

An overview of *TRACES* co-creation journey is presented in the following scheme. At the core of the approach is the idea to use cultural and/or educational activities as co-creation opportunities (Fig. 1).

Details of the activities can be found at the dedicated website IA Spectatrice.[1]

---

[1] www.ia-spectatrice.net [1].

2 Ecosystem, Context and Challenge Addressed

2.1 *External Context and Ecosystem*

The policymaking and scientific community dealing with AI have stressed the importance of transparency, intelligibility and accountability in the social acceptance of artificial intelligence. Society needs to increase its understanding and awareness of machine learning to engage in a democratic debate about the opportunities and risks of its development [2].

As in the case of GDPR, laws are enforced at European level, but until their values become shared and embedded in the general culture, they will not produce the desired effect and will remain out of the control of the lay citizen.

In the meantime, research on Ai and machine learning is advancing at tremendous speed. Many valuable educational activities are being proposed, but tend to focus on equipping the public with basic knowledge about algorithms and artificial intelligence: this is a necessary, but not sufficient aspect. In fact, it neglects the issue of how AI is made visible and recognisable and how it is represented: we believe that these are essential aspects if we want to preserve a capacity to operate informed choices about AI.

2.2 *Organisational Background*

In the last 3 years *TRACES* has initiated several projects using Living Lab approaches, bringing together the science community and other actors from the arts, international cooperation, education, etc.

So far *TRACES'* approach of co-creation is based on the concept of developing public activities within the "grey zone", where the frontier between knowledge production and knowledge dissemination is not well defined [3, 4]. That is, activities that satisfy at the same time the needs of the general public and the needs of the research and innovation community. The Living Lab approach is particularly suited for this idea. The aim is to combine dialogue approaches within public engagement initiatives, and Living Lab methodology and open innovation approaches, to provide meaningful explorations of science based, socially relevant issues. *TRACES* is adapting the usual methods of Living Labs (involving end users in the design/testing) and the classical process of co-creation, exploration, experimentation and evaluation, to events in which the general audience with a cultural interest/involvement in the issue can participate.

TRACES believes that one of the most interesting aspects of co-creation is the possibility to *satisfy at the same time independent agendas*. This is different from *aligning different agendas*, typical of a more classical form of collaboration. In this case, it means that it is aimed to collaboratively set up a situation that will potentially serve the needs of various participants in many, potentially very different ways.

TRACES proposes to identify these two modes as "collaborative" and "generative".

In the "collaborative mode", co-creation mainly consists in a process of alignment of different stakeholders toward a common goal, in order to collectively achieve a result or find a solution. The prototype in these cases is focused on the solution.

In the "generative mode", co-creation is intended as a collectively generated opportunity to help different stakeholders to achieve autonomous goals. Prototyping here is used essentially as a collective exploration: not a solution in itself, but an opportunity and a facilitator to identify several independent solutions. It is thus clearly a radically prototyping-driven approach [5].

The indicators and values that can be used to assess these two modes of co-creation are obviously very different. In the case of "generative mode", the attention focuses on the dynamics among the participants/stakeholders, while in the "collaborative mode" the focus lies on the capacity of the prototype to provide a solution to a specific problem.

The working hypothesis is that the "generative mode" is an appropriate approach in the context of Social Innovation and RRI, the area of exploration of SISCODE.

A second interesting action research question the team was able to address is the relationship between cultural activities and co-creation activities within public engagement and informal education venues such as a Science Centre or Museum.

In recent years an increasing interest of the public engagement community in the world of participation and co-creation, and vice-versa has been observed. Science Centers are integrating Fab Lab spaces and Living Lab approaches in their offer, citizen science activities are increasingly merging with science engagement activities, design thinking and discussion game methods are fertilising each other. This is a promising opportunity of renewal for science communication practices. However, co-construction activities and science culture/engagement activities do not necessarily share the same objectives, neither the same business model. Also, the combination of these two approaches could be influenced by their fashion effect, masking of differences and blurring the clarity of the political value of such activities.

During the entire journey it was aspired to keep the challenge at the border of these two worlds with a twofold objective: enriching the challenge itself by hybridising the two cultures, and exploring the common features and the diversities among them.

The attempt to keep on working at the frontier between cultural activities and co-creation, and possibly blurring this frontier, also strongly oriented the choices of the exploration.

2.3 The Specific Challenge

TRACES' challenge aims at raising the issue of intelligibility of AI, at a time where it has become pervasive of all human activities. How can people enforce their "right to be informed" in automated decision processes using algorithms in everyday life? How can the presence of AI-based support to professional or everyday life decisions become noticeable and readable for end users/citizens so they can make informed choices in crucial aspects of their lives? How can we make people more conscious of automated decision processes/services/applications and of criteria used by algorithms? How can we make ethical issues explicit and understandable for the generic users?

A real need of including discussions on the topic in contexts and situations easily accessible by general audiences, such as in educational or cultural activities has been identified.

Starting from a rather traditional framing of the issue, the co-creation journey led to the identification of a non-explored angle, that is, shifting from AI as subject of cultural and educational activities or as tool for cultural and educational activities, to AI as a target group for educational or cultural products.

3   The Co-creation Journey

3.1   Analysis of the Context

After a preliminary analysis that led to the first statement of the general challenge, *TRACES* adopted an innovative approach for context analysis and reframing of the problem in line with the general principle of working at the frontiers between co-creation and cultural/public engagement activities. This consisted in setting up **an exhibition** to support participatory events and collect inputs form different publics and stakeholders [6].

Participants were involved at different levels: from fully committed, long term engagement participants, to "one shot" contributors who provided their input during a single event.

This phase allowed **the use of an exhibition and a series of public events as a tool for stakeholder analysis, context analysis, stakeholder engagement and idea reframing**.

The outcome of this phase was the precise framing of the problem, as well as the identification of the 5 main communities to be further involved and their most relevant representatives to engage: research, culture, art, civil right activists, policymakers.

3.2   Reframing of the Problem

It became soon apparent that most efforts to explore AI in people's life revolved around two approaches: AI as *subject* of cultural and educational activities or AI as *tool for* cultural and educational activities. That is: *about* AI, or *using* AI. What was missing was cultural and educational activities *for* AI. In other words, it became clear that **it was essential to explore AI as a *target group* for cultural and educational activities**.

After the idea was reframed, two workshops were organised at the Caen "Living Lab festival TURFU" involving scientists, facilitators, and two groups of 25 young people. *TRACES* wanted to ask this question to themselves and the young people in the audience: "since we now know that algorithms are listening to what we do, what do we want to tell them?" The answer took the form of an ideal library of books, films and series, paintings, political slogans and music. In itself an interesting exploration, this ideal library was then used as a boundary object to define the subsequent steps of the journey.

3.3   Envisioning of Alternatives

At this stage of the prototyping sequence it was decided decided to stabilise the co-design team, trying to have a group of people committed to move together until the end of the journey. A very fertile diversity of profiles joined in, and notably Axel Meunier, a PhD student at Goldsmith University (UK) and SciencePo Medialab (France), interested in SISCODE as field study for his doctoral theses on design. His participation was essential to frame the notion of co-spectatorship.

The first of this workshop held on 27th of January 2020 was devoted to exploring and characterising the real-life situation aimed to be described. By using an approach inspired by the service design blueprint [FS7], the team explored different potential bifurcations. This exploration led to define the focus and the prototype in the journey as ""co-spectatorship of a theatre play involving AI and humans".

3.4   Development and Prototyping

On March 10, a workshop was organised in a well-known theatre and cultural venue in Paris, la Maison des Métallos. Participants from various fields (art, engineering, scientific facilitation and communication, research) experienced a situation of co-spectatorship with artificial agents.

Axel Meunier described the workshop with these words: "We are trying to pay attention to the moments of suspension when machines that can hear and see cease to be tools. When we stop being users. When we become public together."

In concrete terms, a short performance was staged, *"Hamlet in the Gym with MTV"*. In an extremely simple setting enriched with objects that can be found in a gym, an actor dictated the famous monologue of Hamlet to his smartphone. Each of the spectators decided to accompany an Artificial Intelligence to see this show. AI were not the unique spectators, nor were they the spectators' "assistants" as they are normally conceived. They were literally brought to the show by the team, as one would have accompanied a child or a disabled person.

The AI participating in the show were the applications **SeeingAI, GoogleLens, Yolo, Camfind, Ava, Voice translator, Teachablemachine, Notes,** and **Robert de Barretin**, an artificial intelligence developed by the art collective DataDADA. Each of the AI, as each of their chaperons, reflected a different perception of the play: some apps just transcribed the text, others translated it in real time or were taking pictures of the show to recognise the objects, while different ones were suggesting shopping choices based on the actor outfit. Besides producing an extremely energetic and creative cacophony (AI don't know how to remain silent during a theatre performance…), the data generated were of extreme richness.

A preliminary analysis conducted by Axel Meunier showed many interesting features. For example, a fluid approach to gender, by privileging simple color codes with respect to evident anatomical characteristics (Google lens often "saw" a woman when the actor was lying on a pink mat, and a male when he was lying on a blue mat). Visual AIs perceived subtle differences that projected a stable situation—a guy on a yoga mat—in very different contexts, such as the world of fitness, or the world of fashion. Details appearing unimportant to their chaperone, were essential for the accompanied AI (e.g., details referring to shopping proposition). This is obvious, but at the same time it is a powerful way to clarify that AI is not there to assist us, but rather to pursue specific, autonomous tasks *while* assisting us.

The situation allowed an explosion of understanding of many non-trivial aspects concerning the relationship with AI. These insights that will inform and enrich each of the participants' professional practices, in many different ways.

It was then decided to organise a **co-creation workshop in which machine learning as a show would be questioned**.

By taking advantage of the artificial co-design team member Robert de Barattin, *TRACES* explored the impact of the presence of an artificial agent among the participants at a zoom meeting to test if people were able to influence Robert's behaviour in the meeting.

3.5   *The Role of Policies and Policymaker Engagement*

The objective is to produce a situation that has an impact through influence. Concerning policymakers, this means that their engagement in the co-creation process should have as effect to widen their understanding of the issue.

The Ile-de-France Region, the Town of Paris, and the university and research leaders were identified as the key policymakers.

Concerning the Ile-de-France Region, the strategy was very successful: the persons in charge of research and scientific culture participated in several events, expressed high appreciation for the approach, and enlarged their views on public perception of AI. This engagement led to the funding of a follow up of the SISCODE challenge, to involve high school students in the period October 2020–June 2021.

Concerning research policymakers, *TRACES* accepted the fact that the respective interests can be different, but still mutually enriching. In fact, it appears that in most cases they accept participation in order to develop an effective outreach tool, rather than to explore the benefits of co-creation for deeper understanding of AI in the social sphere. In a sort of "Trojan horse" strategy, accepting this as a useful collaboration that may provide strong impact in the medium term.

4 Experimentation: Output, Transformations, Outcomes

4.1 Final Concept

The outcome of the exploration is a procedure to support an audience to engage with AI in a live cultural event, thus enabling to discover the way people can live this co-spectatorship.

In very simple terms, the procedure implies assuming a reverse role (identifying ourselves as chaperon for AI to a cultural event), observing a cultural event together with the AI, and analyse how the AI "perceives" the same event.

TRACES tested it in two specific situations (a theater play and a zoom meeting), and will finalise the procedure in 2 additional events: AI observing a science festival (Caen, 9–10 October 2021), AI observing the European Researchers Night (Paris, 29 November 2021) [1].

From the beginning of the project "sustainability" was intended as the continuous, long term change produced in engaged stakeholders. According to this approach, the *product* or the *idea* or the *prototype* do not need to be sustainable. It is their *impact* that needs to be sustainable.

For the specific case, the strategy to ensure **the situation proposed in the workshops is "rich & juicy" enough to produce a progressive change in the way workshop participants and other stakeholders conceive the issue of AI in culture and society**. The question then is: how do we measure this impact? What is the time span to observe? How to identify common indicators, since the impact on each stakeholder might be of very different types? How do we go beyond the purely anecdotal report of the reactions of the participants? How to spot if the participants were indeed influenced by the prototype in their subsequent choices, given that it will surely not be the only agent of change, but just one of several driving forces?

4.2 Transformations Triggered and Outcomes

TRACES as an organisation was deeply influenced by the project. First of all, a deeper understanding of the co-creation process was acquired. This helped to test new approaches, but also helped us make sense of already initiated but not fully understood practices. In other words, together with the introduction of new practices, the level of self-consciousness and reflexivity of the organisation was clearly enhanced.

Secondly, novel forms of collaboration were experienced with a wider variety of subjects, with a direct impact on the networking capacity of the organisation. Thirdly, new competences were acquired that are directly enhancing the credibility of the organisation, both concerning the content (AI in social context) and the form (co-creation). This is easily recognisable in success such as the funding of a continuation of the project at Regional level, or the participation in a EU project applying Living Lab methodology to open schooling (SALL) [7].

5 Lessons Learnt and Reflections

A number of critical as well as highly interesting issues have been identified throughout the experimentation.

At first, the journey offered many unexpected and extremely rewarding creative turns, from a quite standard first enunciation of the challenge to the emergence of a truly innovative and non-standard solution. The team considers this as a genuine proof of the power of co-creation.

Also, making the new approach comprehensible was a challenge in itself, both within the SISCODE consortium and with respect to some of the stakeholders. These difficulties allowed us to identify one of the critical issues on the different roles that a prototype can have in a co-creation process: proposing a terminology to clarify this—a generative mode (the one adopted by us) *vs* a collaborative mode.

Adopting the generative mode presents several difficulties in terms of clarity and concreteness of the outcome. On the other end, it allows to treat each stakeholder differently in terms of the impact and the change generated. This poses tricky but interesting questions to the SISCODE exploration of co-creation.

References

1. IA Spectatrice. www.ia-spectatrice.net. Last accessed 29 Mar 2021
2. Villani C, Bonnet Y, Rondepierre B (2018) For a meaningful artificial intelligence: towards a French and European strategy. Conseil national du numérique
3. Merzagora M (2017) Science centres and science engagement activities as research facilities: blurring the frontiers between knowledge production and knowledge sharing
4. Merzagora M (2016) The grey area: blurring the frontiers between scientific research and science communication. In: PCST 2016 conference proceedings
5. Schrage M (1996) Cultures of prototyping. In: Terry Winograd (ed) Bringing design to software
6. Bron S, Leroy M, Merzagora M (2018) Science centres as research facilities, exhibitions as explorations. Spokes Sci Engagem Mag 38 (2018)
7. https://www.schoolsaslivinglabs.eu

Assessing Co-creation in Relation to Context for RRI Operationalisation

Francesca Rizzo and Alessandro Deserti

Pilot projects and experimentations, especially when conducted in restricted contexts, require assessment activities in order to determine not only their success or failure, but also to identify potential for replication, best practices and obstacles to be tackled in the future. In addition to this, monitoring and assessment have been a pressing issue both in the landscapes of co-creation and RRI, the two main fields that SISCODE operates within. Especially in the field of RRI this issue can be traced back to a gap between the theoretical concepts underlying RRI and their effective transition into practice [4, 17]. The scope of this chapter is reporting on the SISCODE approach to assess the project pilots within the context of co-creation. In the evaluation process, all aspects of the experimentation were considered in order to effectively derive considerations from theory to practice and vice versa.

1 Monitoring and Assessing Co-creation

Like many other participatory activities, co-creation involves a great variety of different actors and stakeholders following a non-linear process [1, 10, 12]. A process that may not have one final result, but rather a variety of less specific, broader directions and future indications as a main outcome [6]. This feature turns its measurement, comparison and assessment into a highly complex procedure, where a variety of elements needs to be taken into account.

F. Rizzo (✉) · A. Deserti
Department of Design, Politecnico Di Milano, Milan, Italy
e-mail: francesca.rizzo@polimi.it

A. Deserti
e-mail: alessandro.deserti@polimi.it

A. Deserti et al. (eds.), *Co-creation for Responsible Research and Innovation*,
Springer Series in Design and Innovation 15,
https://doi.org/10.1007/978-3-030-78733-2_14

Co-creation has been widely discussed as an approach that provides access to new and to date unused resources to co-create value for both business and society [3, 6, 14].

Nevertheless, a lack of directions has been identified regarding the set up of a specific strategy to embed co-creation; analogously, there are missing indications on how to effectively apply co-creation for business purposes [6, 14]. This lack can be partly traced back to the not well-defined characteristics, techniques and methodologies that shape the specific value of co-creation [6, 17].

The need to situate co-creation in an explicit scheme and frame in order to be able to assess its success later on [17] has been addressed in SISCODE by conducting 10 experimentations which were informed according to a specific definition and framework for co-creation while furthermore addressing the aforementioned common issue: trying to close the gap between theory and practice [18].

Moreover, the entire reasoning on the assessment of co-creation goes beyond its use for proving efficacy and evaluating the overall activity. It has also suggested that the activities of assessment and evaluation contribute in building awareness and knowledge. The importance to integrate them into the activities of co-design and co-production derives from this assumption, since they can eventually lead to an improvement of the created solutions, increase motivation among the participants and lead to perceived additional value [5].

The additional dimension of the creation of long-term value in the shape of organisational capabilities and new strategies [6] that may be triggered by the introduction of co-creation exploring a broader level of impact is to be addressed specifically in this chapter.

2 The Issue in Assessing RRI Initiatives

RRI has been identified as an opportunity to tackle global societal challenges by 'anticipating and assessing potential implications and societal expectations with regard to research and innovation, with the aim to foster the design of inclusive and sustainable research and innovation'.[1] Even though it has been widely discussed in theory, there is still a lack of its translation into practice, especially regarding evidence of impact in empirical settings [2, 7–9, 16]. This lack of application in real settings could be traced back to missing proof of impact and benefits leading to hesitation in adopting the novel approach despite its promising prospect [7, 8, 16].

Especially the MoRRI project[2] (Monitoring the evolution and benefits of Responsible Research and Innovation in Europe) addressed the issue of monitoring the development and evaluate the benefits starting from the five dimensions of RRI (Gender equality, Public engagement, Science literacy and science education, Open access,

---

[1] https://ec.europa.eu/programmes/horizon2020/en/h2020-section/responsible-research-innovation.

[2] http://morri-project.eu.

Ethics, and Governance as an overarching dimension) to develop, following an extensive research, a set of core indicators as well as a number of key insights on which needs to be considered and addressed when assessing RRI initiatives [11].

Some of these key insights to be considered to succeed in the task of monitoring and assessing RRI are not only crucial for defining synthetic indicators. They are also relevant dimensions at stake in shaping different and all-embracing ways of collecting data and defining benefits and KPI's including the perspectives of the involved stakeholders. This implies considering indeed the different stakeholders' point of view as well as the relatively long timespan required to be able to evaluate real change, being aware that the latter requires a certain amount of time reaching beyond the timeframe of most projects [11].

Dealing specifically with the investigation of the potential of co-creation in RRI, one of the main aims of SISCODE is to identify a model of co-creation ecosystems that includes the monitoring, evaluation and prediction of impacts. The inclusion of stakeholders and actors external to the organisation leads to a broader perspective on factors to be considered throughout the process forming an entire ecosystem around the initiative.

3   The Role of the Assessment Framework in the SISCODE Project

The importance of the relations among the single pilots and their role within the general elements addressed in SISCODE came to light relatively early in the experimentation. In particular, it emerged fundamental to include some additional points that were missing in the initially planned task and with the potential to provide precious insights on both the overall impact of the co-creation process (within the organisation, the ecosystem and policy context in which the organisation operates, and the project), and future possibilities.

Furthermore, some other aspects to be taken in consideration emerged.

Firstly, the need and opportunity to use this assessment to evaluate the broader impact of the entire initiative, and not only the single pilots, provided an additional layer of insights, connections and possible overall contributions to the project (Fig. 1).

Secondly, the general lack of evaluation and impact assessment tools in RRI initiatives was detected. It was noted that a number of other projects were tackling the challenge of impact assessment in (RRI) projects developing and testing indicators, processes and tools. The 'Monitoring the evolution and benefits of Responsible Research and Innovation' (MoRRI)[3] project SUPERMoRRI,[4] and a network of other projects dealing with monitoring and assessing shed light on the relevance of an issue affecting the entire field of RRI and even beyond.

---

[3] http://morri-project.eu.

[4] https://super-morri.eu.

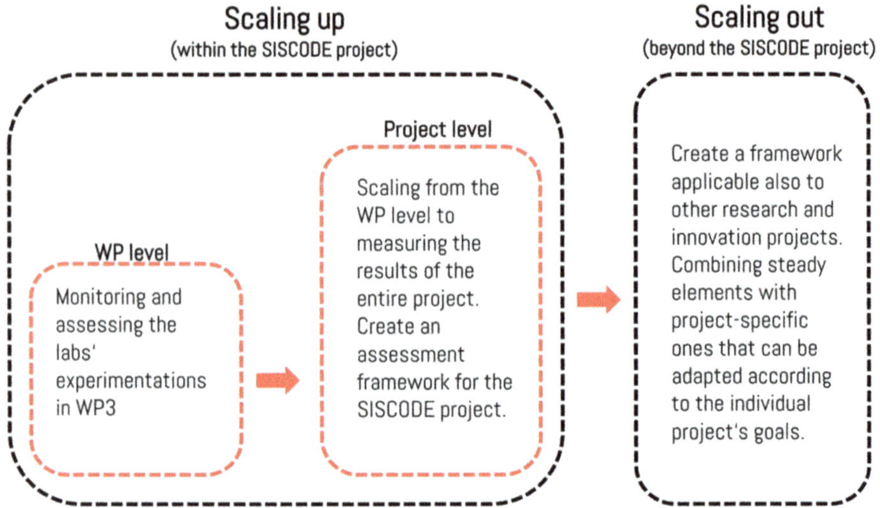

Fig. 1 From scaling up to scaling out

These findings and the resulting shared need significantly impacted on the development of SISCODE assessment framework, as well as on the consideration to scale it out, going beyond the project-level expanding the initially planned task.

As anticipated, the assessment framework was originally planned to be limited to the pilot experimentation. However, the relevance of the topic of assessment within the RRI and STI community that are experimenting with co-creation led to its extension to a broader level, going beyond the project scale (see Chap. 2). The development of an assessment framework considering the different elements and fields that RRI and co-creation imply, and their combination have been essential in order to be able to assess the full dimension of the project's goals.

Co-creation and RRI are the two main pillars that shaped the framework and its tools, together with additional, project-specific indicators derived from studies aimed at providing directions and means for monitoring its impact in different fields among co-creation, RRI, social innovation and design [15].

3.1 Parameters for Assessment

In the light of this, in the following the development of the SISCODE assessment framework, its rationale and underlying concepts are detailed.

A first exploration analysed the existing assessment tools and indicators in the RRI field. The research was intended to build a robust foundation to define a rationale of the general framework based on indicators fundamental for RRI.

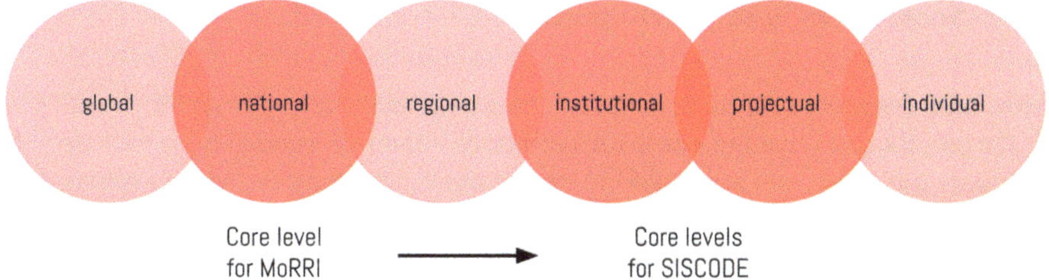

Fig. 2 Scaling down the MoRRI indicators to the organisational level

The investigation led to one of the few specific assessment researches in the field conducted within the MoRRI project that resulted in the definition of a series of indicators to assess RRI initiatives. Because of their rationale and scope, the indicators developed for MoRRI represent one of the two main elements behind the assessment framework of SISCODE. However, operating on a national level, numerous indicators needed to be adapted or downscaled to fit the needs of SISCODE. For example, among the MoRRI indicators, some refer to data from large statistical European datasets, as the Eurobarometer, and a series of complementary studies not applicable to small-scale initiatives. On the topic, deriving from MoRRI, the follow up project SUPER MoRRI[5] project has taken on the task of developing a framework for monitoring the evolution and impact of RRI on a project level. However, the project is still ongoing and its results were not yet available at the time when the SISCODE assessment framework was developed.

Also, the MoRRI indicators focus exclusively on the field of RRI, while the area of investigation of SISCODE includes other disciplines, like co-creation. The extension to other areas implied to enlarge the set of indicators so as to be able to appropriately measure the observed phenomenon. That said, the rationale behind the definition of a set of indicators started from the existing set of MoRRI indicators, which have been selected, reviewed, and, when possible, adapted and scaled to be combined in a new series of project-specific indicators developed individually for SISCODE.

As anticipated, one of the main implications when investigating the indicators developed in MoRRI has been the necessity to review, select and appropriate by downscaling the assessment from the national scale for which it has been elaborated. Considering that SISCODE is operating on a projectual and institutional level, addressing a considerably different dimension (Fig. 2), some of the aspects could not be addressed in their original shape.

---

[5] https://super-morri.eu.

3.2 SISCODE Specific Indicators

SISCODE indicators for assessment have been defined starting from the overall goal of the project and reaching out to the ambition of the experimentation; each specific objective has then been associated to one or more data sources for the evaluation as well as to corresponding indicator(s).

The development of the assessment framework and the definition of the data to gather through it took into account both theoretical and practical concerns, requiring to consider the gap of measurable data which can be obtained just through collection of primary data. Therefore, the assessment framework has been shaped targeting specific areas of interest.

3.3 Areas of Interest

Three main areas of interest have been identified for SISCODE, namely:

3.3.1 Stakeholder Engagement

This first area of interest addresses all matters related to the engagement of stakeholders on different levels. From the documentation of the types of stakeholders involved in the single project to general, organisational strategies for the identification and involvement of stakeholders. It is aimed to examine the quantity and variety of stakeholders involved as well as organisational practices and organisational change in relation to involvement practices.

3.3.2 Co-creation, Its Tools and Methodologies

Co-creation as a field of investigation relates directly to methodologies and tools used in SISCODE. Co-creation is to be investigated from a variety of different angles taking it into consideration as a practice itself when applied in the specific project with a structured methodology and specific tools. Furthermore, it is to be investigated from a broader perspective taking into account the transformation its application may trigger at a project level, on an organisational level and in the entire ecosystem of operation. It is therefore examined both as a practice focusing on its elements, methodologies and tools, as well as a practice that may evolve according to the context of application and the changes it can trigger in this context.

3.3.3 Dissemination

The dissemination of results is to be considered on one hand in direct relation to RRI, exploring the practices of provision of open access to results, and on the other hand as the capacities and practices of effectively communicating results to single stakeholders, communities and policymakers investigating the potential of future developments and impacts, exploiting a variety of channels and tools.

3.4 Transversal Topics

There are specific topics that can be considered as high-level categories, and therefore relevant for the overall project. Their nature associates them with multiple indicators. They underline the transversal aspects and the interconnection among the areas of interest, indicators and their means of analysis. In consequence, it is important to note that the same data can feed more than one indicator, since it can be re-aggregated according to the relation to the topic observed. Hence, the analysis of transversal topics entails to consider more indicators.

The main topics addressed in the investigation are:

3.4.1 (Influence on) Policymaking

The topic addresses a fundamental dimension of SISCODE. Considering the small scale of the experimentation that has been conducted, it is investigated to what extent and with which areas of policymaking these bottom-up initiatives established a dialogue with and were able to make an influence on.

3.4.2 Ecosystem Transformation

Especially when relating to multi-stakeholder involvement and the introduction of co-creation practices, it was investigated to which extent the entire ecosystem surrounding the pilot is influenced.

3.4.3 Organisational Capacities

The organisational capacities of the single labs were investigated starting from (1) the capabilities and knowledge present in the beginning of the project, (2) the ones that have been acquired throughout, (3) the transformative processes that might have been triggered during the project, and (4) the ones that are ongoing beyond its conclusion.

4 SISCODE Assessment Activities

The assessment activities planned, developed and conducted throughout SISCODE can be divided in three levels of evaluation.

4.1 Prototype Scale

At the first level, the assessment within the process of the single co-creation journeys is to be addressed by assessing the prototypes produced. This activity is considered a part of the assessment activity, with a focus more on the process and tools of the assessment rather than its results. For this assessment, the labs have been provided with a set of tools and instructions for application to monitor, evaluate and improve the single prototypes without requesting documentation or quantitative data. The knowledge and eventual capacities acquired in this process are then assessed as part of the levels 2 and 3.

4.2 Pilot and Experimentation Scale

The second and the third levels of analysis are the ones directly connected to the list of indicators. The second level focuses on the achievements of the single pilots. Considering the diversity in size of organisations, available resources, and field of work, the individual accomplishments have been analysed from a qualitative point of view. Pilots achievements have been assessed in relation to the prototype, organisational learnings and new knowledge acquired and finally, transformations triggered in the ecosystem in which the lab is operating. The third level of investigation is taking a broader view on the entire experimentation evaluating insights, opportunities, pitfalls, best practices, and learnings in relation to the set of indicators of SISCODE.

The research on the ground of the framework and its levels of analysis led to the definition and development of different tools concurring to the assessment (Fig. 3). The tools are: the labs' journey spreadsheet, the self-assessment questionnaire, and future scenarios envisioning the long-term impacts of the solutions co-created (Fig. 3).

Because of their nature and scope, such tools are to be considered as partly transversal to the previously described dimensions of (i) stakeholder engagement, (ii) co-creation, its tools and methodologies, and (iii) dissemination, and they are meant to gather and evaluate as much data as possible.

The labs' journey spreadsheet consists of an online shared excel file documenting objectively inputs and outputs and anticipating few outcomes that can be expected to be reached as a result of the concluded activity.

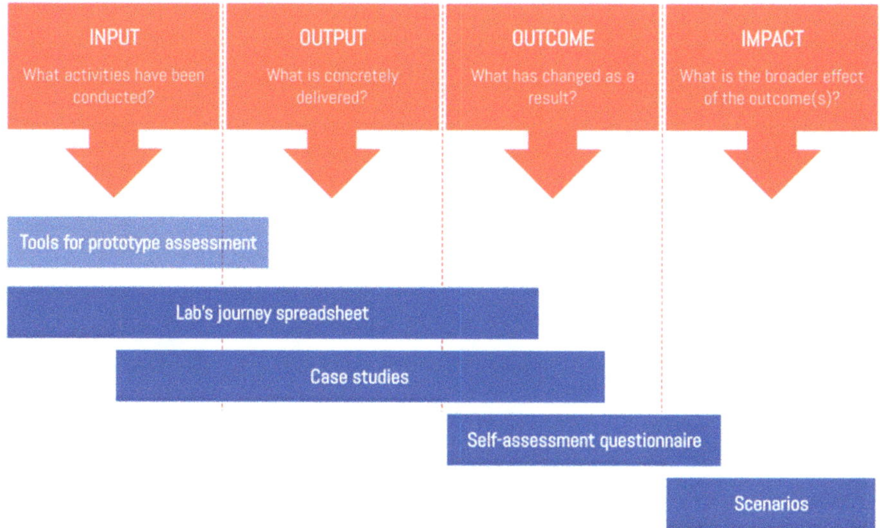

Fig. 3 SISCODE assessment tools in relation to the rationale of the framework

The self-assessment questionnaire focuses on the reflection on the outcomes and mid-term results of the experimentation. They can for instance manifest in new strategies or practices within the organisation, going beyond the single activities and the pilot itself. It aims to trigger also an initial reflection on longer-term impacts that will then be elaborated further in the scenarios. When dealing with complex and unstructured problems, the process itself can lead organisations to re-define, re-learn and unlearn previous knowledge triggered by questioning and reflecting on current practices [13]. In this context, the questionnaire aims to trigger such reflections, and both investigate and nurture organisational learning at the same time [17].

The scenarios are exclusively considering potential impacts on a long-term. Going beyond the time frame of the project, they envision future possibilities (future scenarios), offering an outlook on potential outcomes not yet achieved, but plausible. Such scenarios can have different shapes, from narratives, to moodboards and videos.

Among them, we opted for videos, considering this format an engaging way to expose possibilities, opportunities and new connections. As such, they serve both as a trigger for further reflections and considerations on the concluded experimentation, as well as to disseminate the pilots' results with a future vision, illustrating what the prototype could become in the future.

All tools described above have been allocated to the series of SISCODE indicators. This allocation is based on the nature and typology of data collected through the single tools. Table 1 shows the specific indicators identified for each area of interest, its means of analysis, and the typology of data collected (qualitative or quantitative data).

The results of the assessment are considered on different levels:

Table 1 SISCODE indicators and allocated tools of assessment

Area of interest	Specific indicator	Means of analysis	Kind of data collected
Stakeholder engagement	Strategies for stakeholder engagement	☐ Spreadsheet ☒ Questionnaire ☐ Scenarios ☐ Case study	☒ Qualitative ☒ Quantitative
	Identification of relevant actors	☐ Spreadsheet ☒ Questionnaire ☐ Scenarios ☒ Case study	☒ Qualitative ☒ Quantitative
	Number of stakeholders involved throughout SISCODE	☒ Spreadsheet ☐ Questionnaire ☐ Scenarios ☒ Case study	☒ Qualitative ☒ Quantitative
	Variety of stakeholders involved	☒ Spreadsheet ☒ Questionnaire ☐ Scenarios ☒ Case study	☒ Qualitative ☒ Quantitative
	Level / role of the stakeholders involved	☐ Spreadsheet ☒ Questionnaire ☐ Scenarios ☒ Case study	☒ Qualitative ☒ Quantitative
	Level of involvement	☒ Spreadsheet ☒ Questionnaire ☐ Scenarios ☒ Case study	☒ Qualitative ☒ Quantitative
	Phases of involvement	☒ Spreadsheet ☒ Questionnaire ☒ Scenarios ☒ Case study	☒ Qualitative ☒ Quantitative

(continued)

Table 1 (continued)

	Frequency of involvement	☒ Spreadsheet ☒ Questionnaire ☐ Scenarios ☐ Case study	☒ Qualitative ☒ Quantitative
	Gender dimension of stakeholders involved	☒ Spreadsheet ☐ Questionnaire ☐ Scenarios ☐ Case study	☒ Qualitative ☒ Quantitative
Co-creation	Frequency of application of co-creation methodologies and tools	☒ Spreadsheet ☒ Questionnaire ☐ Scenarios ☐ Case study	☒ Qualitative ☒ Quantitative
	Typologies of co-creation tools applied	☒ Spreadsheet ☒ Questionnaire ☐ Scenarios ☐ Case study	☒ Qualitative ☒ Quantitative
	Processes and strategies for the application of co-creation	☐ Spreadsheet ☒ Questionnaire ☐ Scenarios ☐ Case study	☒ Qualitative ☒ Quantitative
	Evaluation of outcomes of co-creation activities	☒ Spreadsheet ☒ Questionnaire ☐ Scenarios ☐ Case study	☒ Qualitative ☒ Quantitative
	Actor satisfaction in co-creation activities	☐ Spreadsheet ☒ Questionnaire ☐ Scenarios ☐ Case study	☒ Qualitative ☒ Quantitative
	Evaluation of co-creation methodologies and tools	☐ Spreadsheet ☒ Questionnaire ☐ Scenarios ☐ Case study	☒ Qualitative ☒ Quantitative

(continued)

Table 1 (continued)

	Application of prototyping methodologies and tools	☒ Spreadsheet ☒ Questionnaire ☐ Scenarios ☐ Case study	☒ Qualitative ☒ Quantitative
	Testing and evaluation of prototypes	☒ Spreadsheet ☒ Questionnaire ☒ Scenarios ☒ Case study	☒ Qualitative ☒ Quantitative
	Considerations on potential for scaling and replication	☐ Spreadsheet ☒ Questionnaire ☒ Scenarios ☒ Case study	☒ Qualitative ☒ Quantitative
	Influence on policymaking	☐ Spreadsheet ☒ Questionnaire ☒ Scenarios ☒ Case study	☒ Qualitative ☒ Quantitative
	Dimension of organisational transformation	☒ Spreadsheet ☒ Questionnaire ☒ Scenarios ☒ Case study	☒ Qualitative ☒ Quantitative
Dissemination	Dissemination of results across media	☒ Spreadsheet ☒ Questionnaire ☐ Scenarios ☒ Case study	☒ Qualitative ☒ Quantitative
	Provision of open access	☒ Spreadsheet ☒ Questionnaire ☐ Scenarios ☐ Case study	☒ Qualitative ☒ Quantitative

1. On an internal, project-specific level to assess the pure functionality of the prototype itself;
2. On an organisational level to measure eventual changes and transformations that the experimentation might have triggered as well as reflecting on potential future impact; and lastly,
3. On investigating the regulatory and policy context to capture transformations and trace them back to actions, activities and strategies put in place throughout the project.

5 Results of the SISCODE Assessment Activities

The next sections present the results of the assessment activities, structuring them according to the three levels introduced above: prototype, organisational, and relation to the ecosystem.

5.1 *Evaluation Results of the Prototypes*

The assessment of the prototypes as a co-creation practice has been considered as a source of data in the indicators (see Table 1), and as such they provided valuable insights for their potentialities in terms of improvement, scaling and replication. Thus, at the prototype level, the focus of the assessment has been on the previous and developing capacities related to prototyping and its assessment, and its impact within the labs.

The most important ones are detailed in the following.

5.1.1 Validation of the Concept

The main scope of the prototyping activities planned from the beginning was the validation of the concept developed in a context where multiple stakeholders and policymakers participated in validating those solutions. The data collected showed that the co-creation activity nurtured in-depth of needs and encouraged further discussions with all the stakeholders involved in the development of the solution. Also, the importance of including policymakers as part of this validation has been stressed: their broader-scale perspective on the complex ecosystem in which the solution is situated often provided a realistic and holistic view on the concept and on what its insertion in a real-life context may lead to.

5.1.2　Testing of Specific Aspects of the Prototype

Especially when considering the testing of complex prototypes and concepts, the testing of their essential aspects in a separate way has been proven effective. Key elements could be tested and verified without having to simulate the entire concept. For instance, in the case of FabLab Barcelona that developed an entire system to fight food waste, it has been crucial to be able to test the single aspects separately since the set-up and testing of the entire ecosystem would have been on one hand not feasible and on the other hand being planned as a set of elements to be composed to build a system it provided precious insights on the single elements and how they could be implemented apart from one another as well.

5.1.3　Reflections on Future Developments

Particularly relevant has been the opening of a constant dialogue with the participants on the current state of the prototype that eventually transformed into a broader reflection both on future developments of the prototype, and the activities of the lab within its ecosystem. Engaging different stakeholders and actors from within the organisation in the process provided support in the development of a sustainability strategy inclusive and conscious of external voices, opinions and considerations.

One unexpected element is then the theoretical reflection on the background of the pilot, which has been traced back to its origins in theory. Thanks to the close collaboration with researchers who participated in the discussion of the prototype and its underlying concepts, the reflection extended to a different, theoretical level, bringing another valuable point of view in a receptive moment of the development. This condition led to bridge the gap between theory and practice, creating a fertile space of constructive discussion.

5.1.4　Experimentation of New Tools

For the monitoring, data collection and assessment of the prototypes, new methods and tools as semi-structured interviews, observation techniques and user tests have been introduced, adapted and applied. This not only produced results for the assessment itself, but also triggered new fields of application for co-creation, going beyond context analysis, ideation and prototyping by fully integrating it into the repetition of prototyping loops. Analogously, the multidisciplinary tools introduced for gathering of qualitative data encouraged an objective documentation of inputs and outputs and a reflection on their functionality and application.

5.1.5 Considerations on Scaling/Replication

Being held open to collect spontaneous and personal feedback from the participants, some users and stakeholders did not only evaluate the prototype but directly made considerations on possibilities to scale the concept or replicate it in different contexts. Taking another point of view and enriching considerations already elaborated in the labs with external voices emerged as an additional opportunity to identify hidden potential of the prototypes and reflect collectively with stakeholders and actors.

5.1.6 Novel Relations and Amplification of Network

Involving a wide variety of users and stakeholders actively in the aforementioned procedures, new connections and contacts in the ecosystem opened further possibilities for future collaborations or further development of the prototype. This awareness resulted clearly from the results of the assessment, since the labs reported on the collaborations and exchanges activated with the stakeholders involved in the co-creation and testing of their solutions.

5.1.7 Capacity Building for Feedback Collection

By providing and suggesting specific tools together with instructions for their application, a learning-by-doing process has been unleashed leading to new capacities built in relation to planning, adaptation and application of tools for assessment.

In conclusion it can be said that the assessment of the prototypes as an activity did not only contribute to the improvement of the concepts themselves, but opened up a variety of benefits and reflections beyond the sheer assessment of the developed concepts. The analysis of the data gathered showed that benefits range from the building and distribution of new capacities to the strengthening of connections with existing and novel stakeholders and eventually shedding light on undiscovered future opportunities.

5.2 Elaborating Results from the Labs

The data collected showed that the co-creation process brought several results at various levels. Figure 4 presents an overview of the main transformations that each lab experienced during SISCODE, the insights at its base have been extracted from the spreadsheet, the self-assessment questionnaire and the case studies. The different main achievements are grouped, and they are associated with those labs who experienced them, the achievements extracted are all related to the main themes of investigation as policymaking, stakeholder engagement and co-creation.

Table 2 provides a detailed account of all the achievements and changes experi-

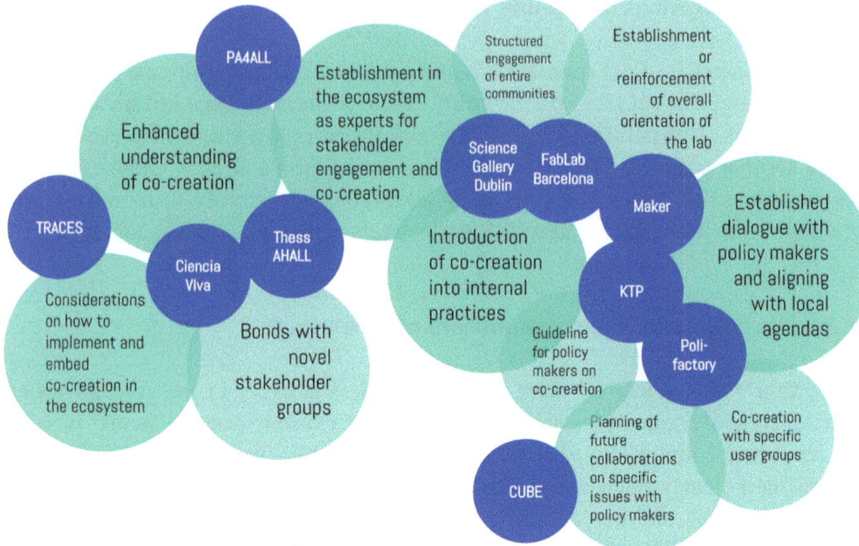

Fig. 4 Overview and synthetic representation of achievements and transformations

enced and reported as directly related to the prototype dimension, in terms of knowledge transfer and organisational change, as well as transformation at an ecosystem level.

5.3   Results of the Overall Pilot Experimentation

The pilot experimentation as a whole has been assessed mainly in qualitative terms according to the indicators.

The results are first reported as a synthetic map of the insights (Fig. 5) obtained to be then described, grouped, and displayed within the previously defined main dimensions and topics acknowledging and pointing out their interconnection and interdependencies.

5.3.1   Stakeholder Engagement

A crucial point in the engagement of stakeholders for the experimentation has been the transition from a less structured approach towards the embedding of strategies for stakeholder engagement into the organisation. This included also setting up initial strategies for individual initiatives that are assessed and adapted throughout the process depending on its development and unforeseen changes.

Table 2 Achievements of the pilots

Lab	Main achievements directly related to the prototype	Developments within the organisation	Changes within the ecosystem
KTP	• Development of two prototypes, both to be implemented and with planned long-term implementation • Empowerment of interactive bonds with academia • Air Protection Programme officialised and released as a document • Platform currently under testing/development for final release	• Introducing co-creation to non-obvious areas of social intervention and other projects • Use of co-creation methodology in internal organisational work • Introduction of an internal team responsible for co-creation established in the organisation	• Strengthening the position of living lab, recognition of the co-creation as a good cooperation practice among different stakeholders • The power of citizens perspective, know how & experience • Exploitation of synergies & horizontal approach • Increase of trust of the regional policy makers in the effectiveness of co-creation and readiness to be adopted in other areas of regional development
PA4ALL	• Development and real-life testing of a new module for the curriculum for agricultural schools in Serbia • Considerations on future integration in the official curriculum	• Enhanced understanding of co-creation	• Raised awareness on the necessity to improve the current curriculum among policymakers
Thess-AHALL	• Pilot programme for a new learning methodology • Novel and stronger bonds with stakeholders	• New and structured strategies on policymaking and stakeholders' engagement • New approaches of running co-creation in a more systematic way and assess its impact in the different steps of the process	• Spread the value of "co-creation & citizens' science" in the City & the University • Stronger bonds and trust with and among different types of stakeholders

(continued)

Table 2 (continued)

Lab	Main achievements directly related to the prototype	Developments within the organisation	Changes within the ecosystem
FabLab BCN	• Creation of a system to fight food waste locally to be replicated and scaled • Overall attraction/direction of the lab towards biomaterial, bio-economy and circular economy • Reinforcement of the Fab City/ Distributed design model	• Increased autonomy and integration among members of the organisation, recognition of the importance to address barriers in terms of financing, spaces and access • Redefinition of the role as interface between local and global • Improvement of skills and diversity of figures working with co-creation • Structuring of the approach for community- and multi stakeholder engagement	• Improved interactions with and within the ecosystems • Improved perception of the context and its complexity • Recognition of the diversity of stakeholders and development of different approaches for the various actors
Maker	• Strengthening of orientation of the lab towards circular economy • Set-up of a new network of stakeholders • Activation of an actor network and development of a set of supporting tools	• Acquisition of new capacities within the lab • New strategies for future projects and initiatives	• Establishment of a solid network for scaling and replication • Strengthening of partnerships and the entire network created • Facilitator among actors in the ecosystem
Poli-factory	• Improvement of skills in co-designing with vulnerable users • Skills acquired in co-creation with children	• Improved multidisciplinarity • New capacities in co-creating with children • Development of approaches for co-designing with vulnerable users	• Improved multidisciplinarity within in the network • Formed and strengthened new bond with and among actors

(continued)

Table 2 (continued)

Lab	Main achievements directly related to the prototype	Developments within the organisation	Changes within the ecosystem
Cube Design Museum	• Interest from participating co-design expert to further use and develop the canvas in future projects and challenges	• Considerations on how co-creation can and will be integrated in the new organisation after a forced restructuring	• Request from involved actors/policymakers to carry out workshops for capacity building • Hesitation to really implement different ways of working triggered by the pilot
Ciência Viva	• Novel bonds with local policymakers and schools • Distribution of material for replication	• Using generic principles and tools of co-creation for internal processes • Raised awareness of the potential of co-creation • Recognition of the need for training	• Generative power of prototyping: new bonds between partners beyond the lab
TRACES	• Trigger to a paradigm shift • Protocol to obtain a new point of view and eventually change perception	• Acquisition of new internal practices • Spread of the application of co-creation practices to other projects • Opened up diverse way of thinking	• Opportunity to feed with new content links with policymakers • Issue of ownership within the ecosystem slows down transformations
Science Gallery Dublin	• Restructuring/reorganising programme to involve young people and co-create programming • Novel relationships with schools in the community • Bonds with research groups, and new experience in working with university partners to evaluate impact of project	• Integration of co-creation practices /SISCODE toolkit also in other projects • Spread of practices beyond the project	• Raised interest of international public and research community • Trigger for considerations on scaling and replication

Furthermore, the variety and individuality of stakeholders have been pointed out several times relating to the need of employing different approaches of involvement within the same initiative, as well as of conducting encounters favouring exchanges and fruitful debate. Especially in relation to the perception among stakeholders, this benefitted from including a facilitator and mediator able to break schemes and allow

Fig. 5 Graphical representation of overall results and insights

encounters of individuals instead of established groups, involuntarily entering the discussion of biases.

It has been found necessary to keep stakeholders involved throughout the entire process to obtain the best possible solution requiring a consistency in motivation that can be achieved by transparency, creating and fostering shared values, setting common goals, and lining out balanced benefits and efforts while aligning expectation from an early stage. Not only motivation and theoretical availability, but also active involvement and efforts have to be managed shedding light on the crucial point of being transparent on efforts expected and potential benefits obtained to manage expectations and avoid misunderstandings and discrepancies.

However, it has been identified that this level and consistency in engagement can only be planned to some extent previously, but partly needs to be co-created, aligning availability and requests, and planning specific commitments without imposing involvement or contributions. In this regard, a potential supporting factor in both engagement and active involvement of stakeholders is the collaboration with similar initiatives, as well as the connection to local and regional agendas to team up to pursue common goals.

5.3.2 Policymaking

The connection to local challenges and their stakeholders is closely related to the influence and impact on policymaking. A key finding from the experimentation is the necessity to align towards common goals and activities with local policy agendas aimed at similar achievements. This can be done by tackling specific challenges addressed by local or regional agendas and/or by specifically choosing policymakers involved according to their orientation. This strategy favours the creation not only of shared objectives but of values and ideas.

Another way to increase impact on policymaking, especially in cases of smaller organisations and initiatives has been identified in exchanging practices, contacts with other organisations and initiatives. Cooperation and collaboration emerged as fundamental to increase potential impact by multiplying resources and maximise the advantages drawn from events and gatherings.

5.3.3 Dissemination

The topic of dissemination is interconnected and complementary to the one of policymaking. The definition of strategies should not only aim at disseminating results in general, but it should point at developing tailored approaches to disseminate findings and results to the different target groups identifying and exploiting their associated channels. Then, apart from the integration of practices to provide open access to results, a variety of broader reflections on the use and results of dissemination activities have emerged.

Dissemination can turn into a means of keeping stakeholders, and specifically policymakers, up to date and aligned. Dissemination itself can be strategically designed and applied as a different way of involving them, defined as 'active dissemination' by one of the pilots.

Also, the dissemination across a variety of channels has been identified in the possibility to share not only the process and results of an initiative, but also considerations on replicability together with instructions and material that enables others to replicate and experiment the developed solution in other contexts. This has been recognised as a different way of sharing knowledge and spreading the heritage of co-creation initiatives. It can furthermore serve as a bridging element for encouraging dialogue and exchange with similar realities. The dissemination of the co-creation practices and tools, showing their application and impact can stimulate adoption and adaptation of co-creation practices by other realities. Moreover, keeping an open and fruitful exchange encourages reflection on best practices, also favouring reflection on context dependency in the light of cultural, institutional and thematic backgrounds.

5.3.4 Organisational Capacities

The learning and exchange on co-creation practices refer mainly to the dimension of organisational capacities and their development and the deriving transformation of an organisation. In SISCODE it has been investigated especially in relation to co-creation and stakeholder engagement throughout the co-creation journey. The findings gathered are mainly associated with acknowledging that real change takes an amount of time that goes beyond the time frame of a project. However, there is first evidence on the embedding of novel organisational capacities and resulting ongoing transformations.

The major insights from this observation are that concrete projects constitute the ideal space where to initiate a learning-by-doing process that gives a tangible shape and results within the boundaries of an abstract concept as co-creation. In doing so, it facilitates the understanding and uptake of practices. This often leads to a conflict with existing practices requiring a transitioning process including a shift of mindset in order to be integrated. This has been found to be facilitated when the new practices to be adopted are also shared, discussed, familiarised with, and to a certain extent appropriated in internal meetings creating a safe space for capacity building, experimentation and discussion. Furthermore, it may lead to a more structured application of already present methodologies including them in planning and strategic activities. A series of capacities related to digital and remote working have been built due to the Covid-19 pandemic SISCODE techniques and tools were revised and adapted for being used online, and became facilitators and triggers to support the learning process and the acquisition of those capacities. The conduction of workshops online as well as the application of the revised tools and methods for online use have led to further minor adaptations intended for better meeting the needs of different user groups.

5.3.5 Co-creation

One of the main insights related to co-creation during the experimentation is its interconnection with all the other dimensions, especially the one of stakeholder engagement. This has to be considered within the frame of the context where it is applied, and the individuals involved. Hence, not only in terms of the overall concept, but as a very individual factor, that can entirely change its application depending on the context and the people involved.

The flexibility of co-creation has not only been pointed out as a positive aspect, but also as an attention point to be taken into consideration in terms of having to deal with the uncertainties of an open-end process within the organisation. In this regard, another point is related to how to manage expectations of stakeholders giving concreteness to an open and transforming process. The co-design-tools applied in SISCODE, deriving mainly from the fields of design and social innovation [12], have been found essential to contribute to this concreteness as well as to build better human interactions both while setting co-creation activities, and during their unfolding. This aspect has been pointed out in relation to a set of necessary soft skills, such as empathy, that appears fundamental in relation to the effective application of co-creation, and that can entirely change the outcomes. This aspect highlights the importance of the human factor, and the necessity to build specific capacities for co-creation beyond the application of tools and methodologies. This learning process has been fostered significantly in cases where co-creation was experimented also internally in the organisation leading to capacity building (like stated in the previous paragraph).

5.4 Discussion of the Evaluation Results Against SISCODE Theoretical Base and Findings to be Further Investigated

The findings detailed in this chapter consider the overall assessment conducted within SISCODE, reflecting on bottom-up experimentations that apply co-creation practices in RRI. A series of key insights obtained during the evaluation in relation to co-creation in RRI for policymaking are detailed in the following.

5.4.1 Extended Role of Stakeholders

Stakeholders and actors appear to be experiencing a shift of their role not only by taking an active part in co-creation activities, but starting to be involved even before the beginning of the initiative, as a part of the entire set-up. However, their active involvement as well as their contributions and benefits need to be planned and assessed apart, in order to increase consistency and arrangement. This means eventually requiring a preliminary involvement for aligning expectations and commitments. These aspects have often not been considered from the beginning, but they emerged during the co-creation process underlining the importance of the role that stakeholders play beyond their direct contribution to the ideation and development of the prototype.

5.4.2 Variability and Fluctuation of Stakeholders' Roles in Bottom-Up Initiatives

Due to the nature of the co-creation activities as being entirely open-ended, the roles and therefore levels of engagement and involvement of stakeholders may change throughout the process. This demands for a regular check and evaluation of the initial mapping of stakeholders and their roles within the process. As part of the self-assessment, labs have been asked to upload their current stakeholder map in the beginning and the end of their journey. The request served the twofold function of providing valuable material for drawing some conclusions in terms of evolution of the stakeholder engagement through time, and also served to lab themselves as

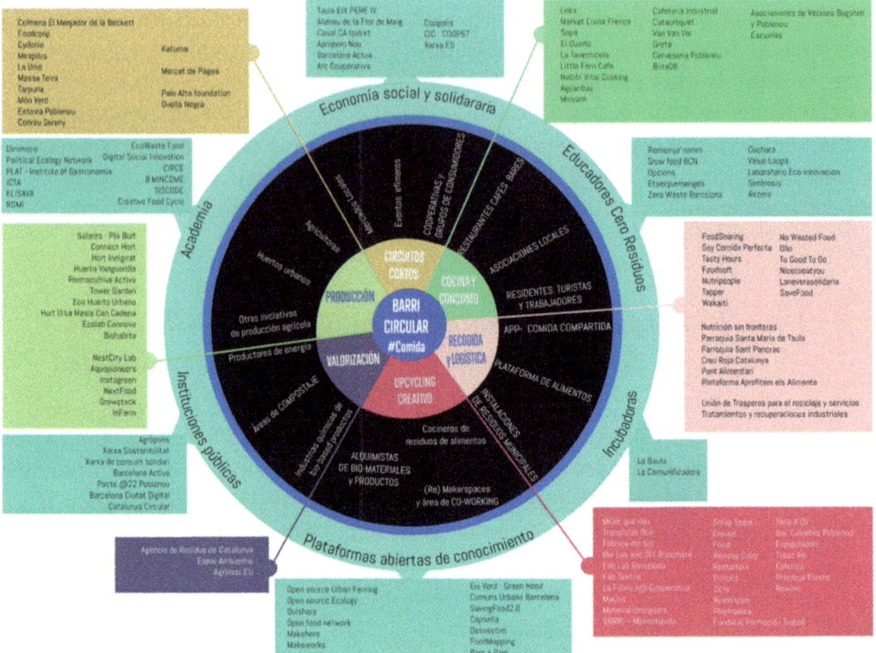

Fig. 6 Stakeholder map of FabLab Barcelona in the beginning of the co-creation journey

a means of reflection. Mapping the stakeholders in two different moments of the process allowed them to observe changes, transformations, and even shifts of roles. The two figures below present the two stakeholder maps from FabLab Barcelona as one example, clearly illustrating this development (Figs. 6 and 7).

5.4.3 Integration of Novel Organisational Practices in Relation and Through Co-creation

The building of new capacities and capabilities in relation to co-creation within the field of RRI through the experimentation conducted in SISCODE was part of the initial goals and dimensions of investigation.

Figure 8 shows the assessment of relevant practices present in the organisation, traced throughout the experimentation and after its end, and displayed in form of averages. The graph represents only the sheer presence of the practice in the organisation, not taking its level or frequency of application in consideration. That said, it is noticeable the presence of a difference particularly in terms of capacities related to co-creation: a slight overall increase and alignment of capabilities has been observed, particularly in the field of co-creation closing the initially identified gap between theory and practice. This can be traced back both to the learning-by-doing effect

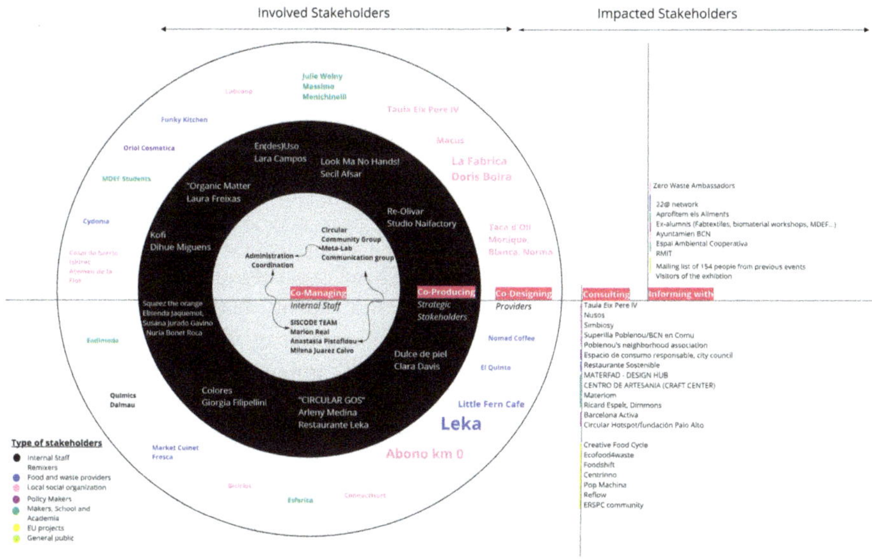

Fig. 7 Stakeholder map of FabLab Barcelona after the conclusion of the co-creation journey

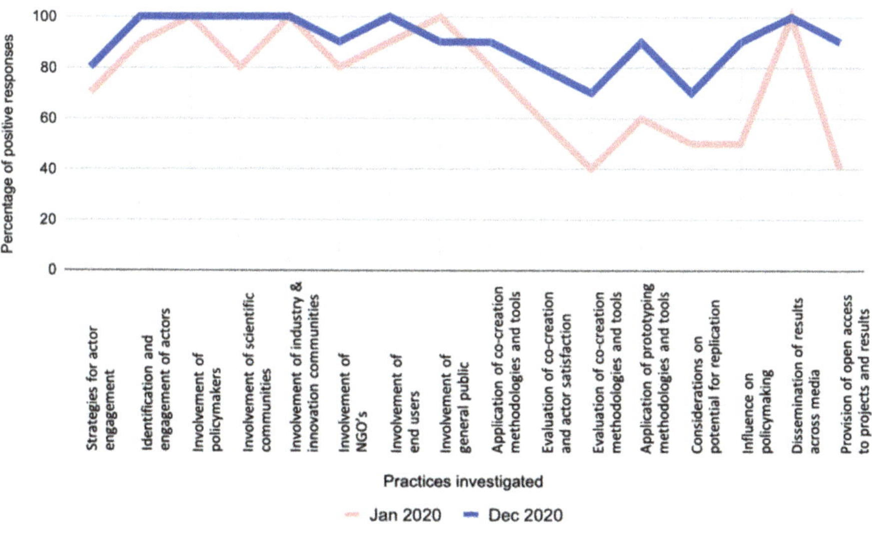

Fig. 8 Percentage of labs with relevant practices present in the organisation

triggered from the application of co-creation, as well as the peer-to-peer learning activities carried out during the project.

By looking at Fig. 8 it is possible to observe that it occurred an acquisition of new practices and capacities where an initial lack has been identified. Then, the diminishing of the value identifying the "involvement of general public" may be associated to the discourse on how the labs changed their perspective on stakeholder engagement in consequence of the application of the strategy and tools proposed in the co-creation process.

5.4.4 Transformative Nature of Co-creation

Considering and assessing the capacity to trigger organisational change, some of the pilots have made broader reflections on the transformative capacities of co-creation taking place both within the single organisation as well as within the entire surrounding ecosystem. This not only included the potential of implementing new practices but also revising the ways in which people within the organisation and stakeholders relate to each other. This could be traced back on one hand to the aspect of co-creation to revoke current power relations valuing different kinds of knowledge and capacities. One the other hand, co-creation itself requires stakeholders, actors and users to confront each other and collaborate, opening up novel opportunities for exchange, discussion and learning (peer and beyond), eventually transforming established relationships and shaping new ones.

5.4.5 A Safe Space for Capacity Building

The complexity of capacity building in co-creation has been pointed out several times, especially in relation to the choice, adaptation, and application of its tools and methodologies. These appear to require a certain guidance or knowledge in order to be applied correctly. Moreover, if a learning-by-doing process is combined with other novel practices like novel techniques or environments for stakeholder engagement it bears the risk of being too overwhelming for the acquisition of new capacities. One potential solution for a step-by-step learning process has been identified in the creation of a safe space during internal meetings and activities: an opportunity for experimenting and discussing practices before running into their application, where to explore possibilities and possible issues ahead of time, and without the necessity to deal with the complexity of stakeholders and the development of solutions at the same time.

5.4.6 Tools for Capacity Building versus Capacities needed to apply Tools

In close relation to the previous point lies the risk of not effectively applying tools and methodologies due to the still ongoing process of familiarising with them, or even learning how to use them correctly. A risk that can cause complications in the process and eventually even hinder the building of new capacities. This could potentially trigger a vicious circle that can lead to frustration and slow down the uptake while increasing resistance to the introduction of co-creation. Acknowledging this, previous training for the use of tools has been identified as one possible solution for this building a knowledge base through specific training or application of tools inside the organisation to then expand and embed this knowledge through further application. This initial training has proven to be fundamental during the SISCODE project.

However, it is to be investigated further how this initial risk of failure and frustration can be minimised when introducing co-creation is not introduced into an organisation as part of a project providing this introductory training.

5.4.7 Complexity of Self-Assessment in Relation to Abstract Dimensions

Self-assessment has led, on one hand, to a series of reflections and insights that did not only enrich the evaluation but also did trigger some additional consideration within the pilot experimentations. On the other hand, the complexity of self-assessment has to be acknowledged. Its subjectivity and dependency on a variety of factors has been noticed especially in the self-assessment questionnaire showing inconsistencies in the patterns of self-positioning on the Likert scales. While the self-positioning in the beginning and the end of the experimentation has been relatively high, it experienced a drop in the intermediate evaluation (Fig. 8; see [15]). The hypothesis made by the researchers in relation to this fluctuation is an initial high positioning due to the sheer presence of a practice in an organisation that is then re-considered, resulting in a lower self-positioning after acknowledging the full dimension and complexity of the topic. Once the overall picture and its complexity is then understood and embedded, it leads to a reinvigoration of the investigated practices.

5.4.8 Awareness of Knowledge and Capacities

While the acquisition and transfer of novel knowledge has been mentioned several times being one of the central issues in the self-assessment questionnaire, it shed light on the related issue of awareness of existing knowledge and capacities. The introduction of novel practices did not only question the validity of current ones but also triggered reflections on how established practices are somewhat similar to the new ones, and how they could eventually integrate and complement each other. Especially some specific capacities related to co-creation like the mapping the user journeys or stakeholders are already practiced in different forms and their integration is facilitated by the recognition of those similarities.

6 Directions for Future Investigations

The assessment framework in this report is characterised by the consideration of various aspects of the co-creation process, reaching out to three scales of observations, and enabling reflections that emerge triangulating data from different sources. This nature and scope make the designed assessment framework inherently prone to get scaled out and replicated in other projects. In particular, although rooted in the specific frame of co-creation, the single objectives, areas of interests and the indicators identified can be applied to the general context of RRI, requiring minor review and adaptation.

This is possible because the process of downscaling, reviewing and adjusting was already considered and included in the development of the SISCODE framework assessment. As described in Sect. 3 of this chapter, the indicators used for assessing the 10 experimentations starting from the MoRRI indicators that were developed for monitoring and assessing the impacts of RRI initiatives at a national scale.

The process of translating the MoRRI indicators from the national scale to that of a RRI-related project produced a set of means of verification and measurement already oriented for being replicated outside of SISCODE (Fig. 9). From the very beginning, considerations on an out-scaling of the assessment framework have been indeed made to re-connect the specific framework to the field of RRI.

Given the current state of the art of the framework, further elaborations in a scaling-out direction regard the division in general and project-specific indicators applicable to most RRI projects together with a guide to define, monitor and assess them.

Therefore, the scaling out of the SISCODE framework is currently under development in direct collaboration with other projects, as part of the work done in the SUPERMoRRI project. The identification of this issue from the RRI community has led to the activation of a series of considerations and initiatives that are aiming at the investigation and scaling of assessment frameworks in RRI.

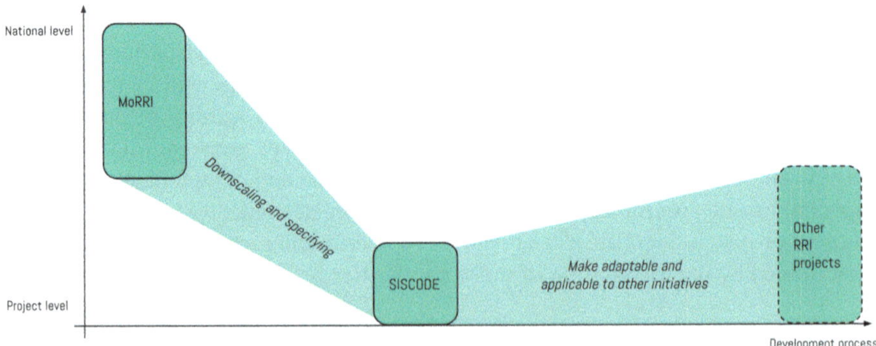

Fig. 9 Potential development process of a general assessment framework

References

1. Deserti A, Rizzo F (2019) Context dependency of social innovation: in search of new sustainability models. Eur Plan Stud 28(5):864–880
2. Deserti A, Rizzo F, Smallman M (2020) Experimenting with co-design in STI policy making. Policy Design Practice 3(2):135–149
3. Deserti A, Rizzo F (2019) Embedding design in organisational culture: challenges and perspectives. In: Julier G et al (eds) Design culture objects and approaches. Bloomsbury, London
4. Emery S, Kendall H, Frewer LJ (2014) Independent evaluation of the public engagement with research and research engagement with society (PERARES) project
5. Foglieni F, Segato F, Sangiorgi D, Carrera M (2019) Evaluating co-production in mental health services as a support for co-design activities. In: Pfannstiel MA, Rasche C (eds) Service design and service thinking in healthcare and hospital management. Springer, Cham, pp 189–209
6. Frow P, Nenonen S, Payne A, Storbacka K (2015) Managing co-creation design: a strategic approach to innovation: managing co-creation design. Br J Manag 26(3):463–483
7. Hansen J, Allansdottir A (2011) Assessing the impacts of citizen participation in science governance: exploring new roads in comparative analysis. Sci Public Policy 38(8):609–617
8. Kurath M, Gisler P (2009) Informing, involving or engaging? Science communication, in the ages of atom-, bio- and nanotechnology. Public Underst Sci 18(5):559–573
9. Loeber A, Griessler E, Versteeg W (2011) Stop looking up the ladder: analyzing the impact of participatory technology assessment from a process perspective. Sci Public Policy 38(8), 599–608
10. Manzini E, Rizzo F (2011) Small projects/large changes: participatory design as an open participated process. CoDesign 7(3–4):199–215
11. Peter V, Maier F, Mejlgaard N, Bloch CW, Madsen EB, Griessler E, Wuketich M, Meijer I, Woolley R, Ralf L (2018) Monitoring the evolution and benefits of responsible research and innovation in Europe: summarising insights from the MoRRI project. Final project report. https://www.technopolis-group.com/wp-content/uploads/2020/02/Final-report-%E2%80%93-Summarising-insights-from-the-MoRRI-project-D13.pdf. Last accessed on 02 Jan 2021
12. Real M, Petsani D, Ajdukovic A, Praça G, Bertrand G, Köppchen A, Machowska M, Wlocdarczyk A, Rasmussen A, Christensen S, Merzagora M, Ghilbert A, Crispell J, Sedini C, Bianchini M (2019) Co-creation journeys. SISCODE deliverable D3.1. https://ec.europa.eu/research/participants/documents/downloadPublic?documentIds=080166e5c11f812a&appId=PPGMS. Last accessed 21 Mar 2021
13. Romme AGL, Van Witteloostuijn A (1999) Circular organizing and triple loop learning. J Organ Change Manage
14. Saarijärvi H, Kannan PK, Kuusela H (2013) Value co-creation: theoretical approaches and practical implications. Eur Bus Rev 25(1):6–19
15. Schmittinger F, Deserti A, Rizzo F, Crabu S (2021) Assessment report. SISCODE deliverable D3.5. https://siscodeproject.eu/wp-content/uploads/2021/03/SISCODE_D3.5_Assessment-report_small.pdf. Last accessed 21 Mar 2021
16. Smallman ML (2016) What has been the impact of public dialogue in science and technology on UK policymaking? UCL University College London, London
17. Zhang X, Chen R (2008) Examining the mechanism of the value co-creation with customers. Int J Prod Econ 116(2):242–250
18. Zwart H, Landeweerd L, van Rooij A (2014) Adapt or perish? Assessing the recent shift in the European research funding arena from 'ELSA' to 'RRI.' Life Sci Soc Policy 10(1):1–19

GPSR Compliance
The European Union's (EU) General Product Safety Regulation (GPSR) is a set
of rules that requires consumer products to be safe and our obligations to
ensure this.

If you have any concerns about our products, you can contact us on

ProductSafety@springernature.com

In case Publisher is established outside the EU, the EU authorized
representative is:

Springer Nature Customer Service Center GmbH
Europaplatz 3
69115 Heidelberg, Germany